EDEXCEL

GCSE Modern World History

Revision Guide

Second Edition

Christopher Culpin, Steve Waugh and Ben Walsh

HODDER
EDUCATION
AN HACHETTE UK COMPANY

Acknowledgements

Photo credits
p. 77 © The body of a German telephone operator in his shelter at the Somme, 1916 (b/w photo), Moreau, Jacques (b.1887) / © Archives Larousse, Paris, France/ Giraudon/The Bridgeman Art Library; **p. 80** 'The Kitchen Is The Key To Victory, Eat Less Bread', 1st World War poster, c.1917 (colour litho), English School, (20th century)/Private Collection/Photo © Barbara Singer/The Bridgeman Art Library; **p. 93** © Archive Photos/Getty Images; **p. 95** © Public Record Office/HIP/TopFoto; **p. 115** © Amoret Tanner/Alamy

Every effort has been made to contact copyright holders, and the publishers apologise for any omissions which they will be pleased to rectify at the earliest opportunity.

Although every effort has been made to ensure that website addresses are correct at time of going to press, Hodder Education cannot be held responsible for the content of any website mentioned in this book. It is sometimes possible to find a relocated web page by typing in the address of the home page for a website in the URL window of your browser.

Hachette UK's policy is to use papers that are natural, renewable and recyclable products and made from wood grown in sustainable forests. The logging and manufacturing processes are expected to conform to the environmental regulations of the country of origin.

Orders: please contact Bookpoint Ltd, 130 Milton Park, Abingdon, Oxon OX14 4SB. Telephone: (44) 01235 827720. Fax: (44) 01235 400454. Lines are open 9.00–5.00, Monday to Saturday, with a 24-hour message-answering service. Visit our website at www.hoddereducation.co.uk.

Cover photo: Civil Rights Marchers with 'I Am A Man' Signs © Bettmann/CORBIS
Illustrations by Barking Dog Art, Peter Lubach and Phoenix Photosetting
Typeset in 11.5/13.5 Garamond by Phoenix Photosetting, Chatham, Kent ME4 4TZ
Printed in India

A catalogue record for this title is available from the British Library

ISBN: 978 1471 831 720

Contents

How to use this book

Explanation and Comment

The main text explains all the content clearly and the Comment boxes provide extra information to put events in context or highlight other issues that you should be aware of.

Key terms

These boxes help you to learn the essential vocabulary by providing you with difficult or new words and giving a definition of their meaning. These are specialist terms that might be used in an exam without any explanation so you need to be able to understand them and use them confidently in your own writing. You could make your own glossary in your notebook.

Revision tasks

Use these tasks to make sure you have understood every topic and to help you record the key information about each topic. These tasks help you to think about the content rather than simply read it.

Exam practice

These boxes provide sample exam questions for each topic. You can check your answers against sample answers online at www.hodderplus.co.uk/modernworldhistory to help to improve your grades.

Exam tips

These tips accompany the Exam practice questions. They give you extra tips on how to answer the questions successfully in order to get the best grades possible.

Key content (end of each chapter)

This is a revision checklist. Be sure you know about each term or phrase in this key content summary. You can also check your knowledge of each topic with our free 'Quick quizzes' which you can find online at www.hodderplus.co.uk/modernworldhistory.

Introduction

You will soon be taking your GCSE in The Making of the Modern World. Your aim is to get the best grade that you can. Our aim in this book is to help you get that grade.

To improve your grade you need to:
- get organised – this book will help you make a revision plan and stick to it
- know the content – this book will help you learn the core content for your course
- apply your knowledge – this book will help you apply what you know to actual examination questions.

How to revise

There is no single way to revise, but there are some golden rules everyone should follow.

1 *Know the objectives of your course:* ask your teacher for full details of the specification. This book is geared to Edexcel's specification A, The Making of the Modern World.

2 *Make a revision plan and stick to it:* start your revision early – the earlier the better. Revise regularly – regular, short spells are better than panicky six-hour slogs until 2a.m.

3 *Revise actively:* be a scribbler; make notes as you learn. You will need an exercise book for most of the Revision Tasks but you can also write in this book.

The rest of this introduction is about how to apply these rules to your revision and make sure that you get the grade you are aiming for.

1. Know the objectives of your course

Assessment objectives for GCSE History

1 *Recall, select and communicate knowledge and understanding of history.*
   You have to be able to recall and select knowledge, and be able to communicate it in a way that shows you understand what you are writing.
   This means:
- using your knowledge of a topic to back up what you say in your answer
- organising this knowledge to answer the question that has been set.

2 *Demonstrate understanding of the past through explanation and analysis of:*
- *key concepts: causation, consequence, continuity, change and significance within a historical context*
- *key features and characteristics of the periods studied and the relationship between them.*

   This means organising your answer in order to:
- show the ability to analyse when this is asked for, rather than to describe
- show understanding of causation, etc.

3 Understand, analyse and evaluate:
- *a range of source material as part of an historical enquiry*
   This means using any kind of material, including photographs, diaries, books, recorded interviews and films from the period you are studying.

   You are expected to:
- extract what is important information from the source
- interpret what is being said and make inferences
- decide how useful or reliable the source is.

● *how aspects of the past have been interpreted and represented in different ways as part of an historical enquiry*
  This means that you have to be able to analyse and interpret how and why historical events, people and situations have been interpreted and represented in different ways.

  You are expected to:
● decide how fair or accurate an interpretation is
● compare different representations of an event.

In all this, remember that the examiner is interested in seeing how much you can think for yourself and apply your knowledge and understanding to the question set.

2. Make a revision plan

You not only need to plan your revision for History, but you need to fit it in with the revision for all your other GCSE subjects. You could use this table to plan your overall revision.

Dates		Revision targets and deadlines			
Month	Week	History	Science	English	Others
Jan	4	Key points summary card for Russia			
Feb	2		Test on metals		
Mar				Controlled Assessment session	

You could then construct another table, like the one below, to plan your History revision. In your plan, aim to come back to each topic several times so that you revise in stages:

Stage 1: Put the date that normal school-based work on a topic is due to be/was completed.
Stage 2: Put the target date for finishing your own summary of the key points for each topic.
Stage 3: Decide when you will give yourself memory tests.
Stage 4: Schedule time for fine-tuning your revision (for example, final memorising work and/or practice examination questions).

History topics	Date	Key points summary	Memory test	Fine tuning
1 Stalin's Five-Year Plans		March	April	2000 Question–May
2 Collectivisation				
3				

3. Revise actively

When faced with revising for GCSE History, most students say:

The ideas in this book are aimed at helping you to remember the core content.

Use the revision tasks in this book

The best way to remember information is to use it – to revise actively. To take an everyday example: to start with it is difficult to remember a new telephone number, but the more you use it the easier it is to remember it.

Throughout this book, you will find revision tasks. Don't miss them out. If you do the tasks you will have to use the information in the book. If you use the information you will remember it better. The more you use the information the better you will remember it.

Use the 'key words' method

Think of your brain as a computer. To read a file on a computer you need to know the name of the file. The file name is the key, and if you do not have this key you cannot get to the file, even though the computer has the file in its memory.

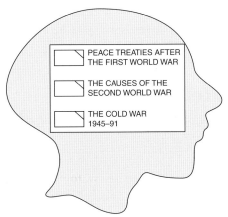

Your brain works in a similar way. When you read something it goes in, but to get the information out again you need the key to unlock your memory. So, one way to jog your memory is to use a 'key words' method. This is how it works.

1   As you read through each paragraph, highlight one or two key words. For example, when answering the question:
    'What were the main political and economic features of the USA during the 1920s?'

●   It had a *democratic system of government*. The President and Congress of the USA were chosen in free democratic elections.

●   It had a *capitalist economy*. Business and property were privately owned. Individuals could make profits in business or move jobs if they wished. However, they might also go bankrupt or lose their jobs.

●   The USA was the world's wealthiest country, but under capitalism there were always *great contrasts* – some people were very rich, others were very poor.

2   You can then use cue cards, or the key content list at the end of each chapter, to summarise your key words for each subheading. In this way you can summarise a whole topic on one sheet.

3   Later on, return to your revision plan and see whether you can recall or rewrite important paragraphs using just the key words to jog your memory.

Other revision ideas

Different people revise in different ways and you may have your own ideas on how to work. Here are some other techniques that students have used.

●   summarising events in diagrams or pictures
●   making a recording of the text and playing it back
●   using acronyms or mnemonics
●   working with friends:
    –   testing each other
    –   comparing your answers to practice questions.

How to succeed in Edexcel Modern World History

You will be examined on three units. Here is a summary of the content and assessment for the three units you will have to study.

Unit	Content	Examination
1	• How did the Cold War in Europe develop? 1943–56 • Three Cold War crises: Berlin, Cuba and Czechoslovakia c.1957–69 • Why did the Cold War end? From Détente (1972) to the collapse of the Soviet Union (1991)	75 minutes *53 marks*
2	One from: • Germany, 1918–39 • Russia, 1914–39 • The USA, 1919–41	75 minutes *54 marks*
3	One from: • War and the transformation of British society c.1903–28 • War and the transformation of British society c.1931–51 • The transformation of British society c. 1951–79	75 minutes *53 marks*

How to succeed in Edexcel Unit I

This is the unit which examines your knowledge and understanding of international relations.

Content

You will need to revise these **three** units:
1 How did the Cold War in Europe develop? 1943–56 (pages 11–20)
2 Three Cold War crises: Berlin, Cuba and Czechoslovakia c.1957–69 (pages 21–25)
3 Why did the Cold War end? From Détente (1972) to the collapse of the Soviet Union (1991) (pages 26–31)

The examination

In this examination, you will answer six questions. The six questions will always be of the same types (see below) and appear in the same order.

Question 1: understanding source material

Give **two** reasons from Source A why relations between the Allies continued to worsen at the time of the Potsdam Conference. *(2 marks)*

- Read the source carefully.
- Pick **two** items mentioned in the source which relate to the question (worsening relations between the Allies) and write a short sentence on each.

Question 2: brief description

Outline **two** issues on which the Allies agreed at the Potsdam Conference. *(4 marks)*

- Describe **one** issue in a short sentence.
- Add a sentence bringing in relevant extra detail which develops the issue.
- Describe the second issue, with extra relevant detail.

Question 3: judging the usefulness of a source

How useful are Sources B and C as evidence of the reasons for the Soviet invasion of Afghanistan in 1979? *(10 marks)*

- Be sure to write about both sources.
- Comment on the usefulness of the sources based on what they say. Do they tell you about the Soviet invasion of Afghanistan? What do they *not* tell you?
- Use the nature, origin and purpose of the sources to comment on their **reliability** or **typicality**.
- Use this evaluation to compare the **usefulness** of each source.

Question 4: brief description of key features

You have a choice in Question 4: answer 4(a) or 4(b).

Describe the key features of the Marshall Plan (1947). *(6 marks)*

- You will need *developed* statements about at least **two** key features: this means giving the feature and then explaining it. Remember this can include causes, events or consequences.

- Ensure your key features are in the right sequence.
- You will get higher marks for more precise explanations.

Question 5: brief descriptions of significance

Explain the importance of **three** of the following in the Cold War:
- The Berlin Airlift, 1948–49
- The Warsaw Pact, 1955
- The Prague Spring, 1968
- The Helsinki Agreements, 1975 *(5 marks for each part – 15 marks)*

- Think carefully and choose the **three** items you know most about.
- Write a brief sentence describing one of the events.

- Add another sentence explaining in detail why it was important in the Cold War.
- Do the same for the other two items you have chosen.

Question 6: essay explaining causation

Explain why relations between the USA and the Soviet Union changed in the years 1980–1985. You may use the following in your answer:
- The Soviet invasion of Afghanistan.
- The election of Ronald Reagan as President of the USA.

You must also include information of your own. *(13 marks)*

- Underline the key items from the question. Here they are: 'relations between USA and Soviet Union', 'changed' and the dates: 1980–85.
- Plan your answer; remember to include a brief introduction and conclusion.
- Don't just *describe* the reason you've chosen, *explain* clearly why it led to *change*.
- You need at least **three** reasons, add one more reason from your own knowledge.

- Develop each reason in detail.
- For best answers, don't just stick with the two items you've been given; add one of your own.
- Make links between one reason and the next. Use link words and phrases such as 'furthermore', 'moreover', 'however', 'in addition', 'as a result of' and 'this led to'.
- Make judgements about the importance of each of your three reasons.

How to succeed in Edexcel Unit 2

This is the unit which examines your knowledge and understanding of **one** of the depth studies.

Content

You will need to revise **one** of the following chapters:

4 Germany, 1918–39 (pages 32–45)
5 Russia, 1917–39 (pages 46–58)
6 The USA, 1919–41 (pages 59–70)

Make sure that you only revise the chapter that covers what you have studied!

The examination

In this examination you will answer six questions.

Question 1(a): an inference question

What can you learn from Source A about Nazi attitudes towards the churches in Germany? *(4 marks)*

This question is asking you to read between the lines of the source and to get a message from the source.
- Make at least **two** inferences.
- Begin your answer with 'This source suggests …'. This should help you focus on the question.
- Support your inferences by reference to the source. In other words, use a quotation from the source.

Question 1(b): a brief description from your own knowledge

Describe the measures taken in the Treaty of Versailles to limit German power. *(6 marks)*

This is asking you to describe at least **two** factors.
- Give the factors.
- Describe the factors, bringing up relevant detail.
- Remember to focus on key words in the question.

Questions 1(c) and 1(d): causation and consequence in context

Explain the effects of the Reichstag fire in 1933. *(8 marks)*

Explain why Hitler carried out a policy of persecution of the Jews and other minority groups in the years 1933–39. *(8 marks)*

- Underline key points in the question.
- Ensure that you focus on causes/consequences. Begin each paragraph by stating the cause and then fully develop each cause you give. Use precise knowledge which will impress the examiner.
- Aim to write about at least two causes/consequences.

- Make links between one cause and the next. Use link words or phrases such as 'furthermore', 'moreover', 'however', 'in addition', 'as a result of', and 'this led to'.
- In your conclusion prioritise the importance of the causes or consequences. In other words decide which was the most important and explain why.

Question 2(a) or 2(b): change

(a) Explain how Germany recovered from its economic and political difficulties in the years 1924–29 under Stresemann's leadership. *(8 marks)*

Or

(b) Explain how the position of young people changed in Germany in the years 1933–39. *(8 marks)*

- Highlight key words, events, dates, etc. in the question.
- You will need to explain a minimum of two changes.
- Aim to write two paragraphs.
- At the beginning of each paragraph focus on the

idea of change, e.g. 'The first change was …'.
- Make a link with the next change.
- Write a conclusion in which you prioritise the changes, e.g. which change do you think was the most important and why OR overall how much change was there?

Planning grid for causes, consequence and change questions:

First factor/change	• Introduce the factor/change • Fully explain it • Make a judgement on its importance • Make a link with the next factor/change *Use link words or phrases such as 'moreover', 'however', 'therefore', 'as a result of', 'this led to', 'consequently'*
Second factor/change	• Introduce the factor/change • Fully explain it • Make a judgement on its importance
Conclusion	• Begin with 'Overall' • Again link the two factors/changes • Prioritise – put the factors/changes in order of importance and explain your decision

Question 3(a) or 3(b): scaffolding question

You will be given a choice of two questions, each of which will have two points (known as scaffolding) to help you answer the question.

(a) Was the effect of reparations the main reason why the Weimar Republic found it difficult to govern Germany in the years 1919–24? Explain your answer.
   You may use the following in your answer:
   ● the effects of reparations
   ● attacks on the Government by left- and right-wing political parties.
   You must also include information of your own.   *(16 marks)*

● Start by making a quick plan for your answer before you write anything.
● Focus on the key words in the question. In this question it is 'why the Weimar Republic found it difficult to govern'.
● Make use of each part of the scaffolding. For best marks, you need to add at least **one** more cause from your own knowledge.

● Remember to make a judgement about the importance of each factor.
● Write a conclusion that gives your overall judgement on the question. Remember, you need to make a decision on the relative importance of all the causes. You could decide that all were equally important or some were more important than others. Give a reason for your judgement.

Planning grid for scaffolding questions:

First paragraph	● Introduce the first reason, which should be the first bullet point. ● Fully explain this reason why the Weimar Republic found it difficult to govern Germany. ● Make a judgement on the importance of this reason. ● Make a link to the second reason.
Second paragraph	● Introduce the second reason, which should be the second bullet point. ● Fully explain why this reason made it difficult for the Weimar Republic to govern Germany. ● Make a judgement on the importance of this reason. ● Make a link to a third reason from your own knowledge.
Third paragraph	● Introduce the third reason. ● Fully explain this reason for the difficulties of the Weimar Republic. ● Make a judgement on the importance of this reason. Some examples of other reasons might be: ● Weimar politicians were blamed for signing the Treaty of Versailles. ● Germany had lost territory under the terms of the Treaty. ● The German people had little experience of democracy and many wanted a return to monarchy. ● The Weimar constitution produced lots of small parties, which led to unstable, changing governments.
Conclusion	● Begin with 'Overall'. ● Make a final judgement on the relative importance of all three reasons.

How to succeed in Edexcel Unit 3

This is the unit which examines your source skills as well as your knowledge and understanding.

Content

You will need to revise **one** of the following three chapters:

7   War and the transformation of British society *c.*1903–28 (pages 71–86)
8   War and the transformation of British society *c.*1931–51 (pages 87–102)
9   The transformation of British society *c.* 1951–79 (pages 103–124)

Make sure that you only revise the chapters that cover what you have studied!

The examination

In the examination, you have to answer **five** source questions.

Question 1: inference

What can you learn from Source A about events at Little Rock High School in 1957?   *(6 marks)*

This question is asking you to read between the lines of the source and to get a message – an inference – from it.
- Make at least **two** inferences.
- Begin your answer with 'This source suggests …'. This should help you focus on the question.
- Support each inference with a quote from the source.

Question 2: source analysis

Study Source C and use your own knowledge. What was the purpose of this representation? Use details from the source and your own knowledge to explain your answer.   *(8 marks)*

- Begin by explaining what the source is suggesting.
- Fully explain the purpose of the source. In other words, what it is trying to make people think or do. Support this with evidence from the source.
- Support the purpose of the source from your own knowledge: what else do you know about the event which adds to this understanding of the *purpose* of the representation?

Question 3: explanation

Use Source C and your own knowledge to explain why the German Schlieffen Plan failed.   *(10 marks)*

- Make a brief plan before you write anything.
- Write a short introduction, listing all your reasons for the failure of the Schlieffen Plan.
- Start with a detailed analysis of the source. What reasons does it suggest for the failure of the Plan?
- Add some details from your own knowledge to support the reason suggested by the source.
- Now write another paragraph, using your own knowledge to give a second reason. Explain in detail how it led to the failure of the Plan.
- Then add a third reason, with a detailed explanation, in a third paragraph.

Question 4: reliability questions

How reliable are Sources D and E as evidence of Haig's ability as a general? Explain your answer using Sources D and E and your own knowledge.   *(10 marks)*

This table will help you to plan your explanation of the reliability and limitations of each source.

	Reliability	Limitations
Content	The source is reliable because of what it tells you about the event or person. It contains facts such as …	<ul><li>It only provides a limited view of the event. It does not tell us …</li><li>It is not accurate because …</li><li>It is mainly opinions, such as …, rather than facts.</li></ul>
Nature	The source is reliable because it is a newspaper, poster, photograph or …	<ul><li>The photograph only gives one limited view of the event.</li><li>The poster/newspaper exaggerates the event.</li></ul>
Who wrote it	It was written by someone whose views are worth knowing. Why?	The author is very one-sided and/or did not witness the event.
When was it written	<ul><li>It was written at the time by an eyewitness. It gives the feelings/views of that time.</li><li>It was written later and the writer had the benefit of hindsight.</li></ul>	<ul><li>It was written at the time and so does not have the benefit of hindsight.</li><li>It was written later and the author has forgotten important events …</li></ul>
Purpose	It reflects the purpose of the author, e.g. propaganda.	It does not give a balanced view because its purpose is to win the support of the reader for …

Question 5: reaching a judgement on an interpretation

Study Sources A, C and F and use your own knowledge.
'Source C suggests that it was their plans for the future which were the reason for the victory of the Labour Party in the 1945 General Election.'
How far do you agree with this interpretation? Use your own knowledge, Sources A, C and F and any other sources you find helpful to explain your answer. *(16 marks)*

- This is the highest-scoring question on the paper, so it will need a planned answer.
- Read the interpretation – the statement in quotation marks – carefully. You need to use the sources and your own knowledge to show agreement **and** disagreement with what the interpretation says.
- You **must** deal with Sources A, C and F because they are listed in the question.
- You can use other sources too if they help your answer.
- For best marks you should evaluate the sources, commenting on their reliability to reach a judgement on whether their evidence is **strong or weak**.
- You should bring in information from your own knowledge which adds to your argument.
- Use the grid below to prepare your plan.

	Agrees with interpretation	Disagrees with interpretation	Strong/weak
Source A			
Source C			
Source F			
Other sources			
Your own knowledge			

Online resources

- This revision guide is supported by representative **example answers** to every kind of Exam practice question from all of the chapters – covering both core and depth content – which are available online at www.hodderplus.co.uk/modernworldhistory.
- Along with the example answers, a **comment** is also given. Reading through these against your answers will help you to build your confidence, improve your answers and, ultimately, your grades.
- **Quick quizzes** are also available online at www.hodderplus.co.uk/modernworldhistory to test your knowledge of the key content. These accompany the Key content boxes found at the end of each chapter, which allow you to tick off each area as you learn them.

During the Second World War, the USA and the USSR had fought together as allies against Germany and Japan. Once this war was won, relations between the two 'superpowers' quickly deteriorated. A new war began – a war of ideas – and so it was known as the Cold War.

Key topics

These are the key topics you need to revise. As with all examination topics you first need to learn the content so you know it well enough to answer a range of questions on this topic.

- Why did the Cold War begin?
- the development of the Cold War, 1945–48
- the development of the Cold War, 1948–56
- Hungary: the tightening of control.

1.1 Why did the Cold War begin?

The Cold War was a new kind of conflict, in which America and the USSR never declared war on each other. Instead there was a stand-off between the two superpowers which included an arms race and a propaganda war.

Conflicting ideologies

The two superpowers had very different **ideologies**.

The USA

What were the main political and economic features of the USA?
- It had a democratic system of government. The President and **Congress** of the USA were chosen in free democratic elections.
- It had a capitalist economy. Business and property were privately owned. Individuals could make profits in business or move jobs if they wished. However, they might also go bankrupt or lose their jobs.
- Americans believed firmly in the freedom of the individual and in government by consent.

In the 1920s and 1930s, the USA had followed a policy of **isolationism**. Now, faced by Communism extending into eastern Europe, the American Government was prepared to help and support people and countries who wanted democratic states with capitalist economies.

Key terms

Ideology: a set of beliefs and characteristics.
Congress: the American representative assemblies (the equivalent of Parliament in Britain). There are two houses, the Senate and the House of Representatives.
Isolationism: withdrawing from international politics and policies.
Supreme Soviet: an elected body of representatives (the equivalent of the British Parliament), but which had no real power. It only met for two weeks a year. It was the Communist Party under Stalin that made the important decisions.

The USSR

The USSR was a Communist state.

- People could vote in elections for the **Supreme Soviet**, but they could only vote for members of the Communist Party and the Supreme Soviet had no real power. In the Communist system, people's lives were controlled closely.
- The rights of individuals were seen as less important than the good of society as a whole.
- The USSR had a planned economy. The Government owned all industry and planned what every factory should produce.

Unlike the USA, the USSR had been attacked many times in the past. Germany had invaded Russia in 1914 and again in 1941. Stalin was determined that this would never happen again. In his view, the USSR could only be safe if the countries on its borders were controlled by Communist governments.

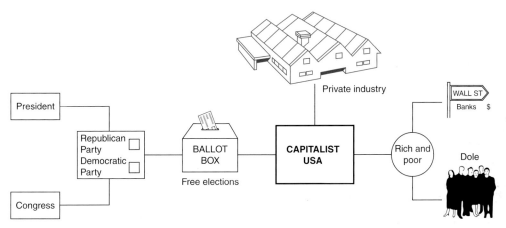

The main political and economic features of the USA.

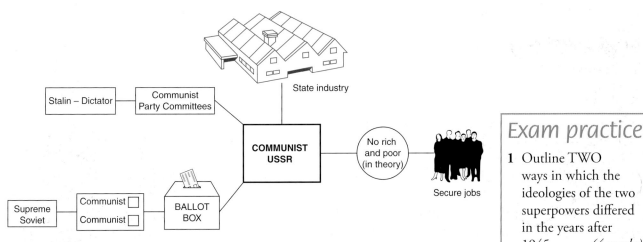

The main political and economic features of the USSR.

Exam practice

1 Outline TWO ways in which the ideologies of the two superpowers differed in the years after 1945. *(4 marks)*

Exam tip The Exam practice question above is an example of a question 2 from Unit 1. You need to:
- give two examples of ways the ideologies of the two superpowers differed
- give one extra sentence for each, giving relevant details.

Revision tasks

1 Choose six key words to summarise the USA's system of government. Then choose six key words to summarise the USSR's system of government.

2 Compare the two in a table with the following headings:

USA	USSR

The breakdown of the Grand Alliance

This was set up in 1941 between Britain, the USA and the USSR to defeat Hitler and the Nazis. It was an alliance of convenience between three superpowers which had little in common.

The Teheran Conference, 1943

At the Teheran conference the Big Three – Stalin (leader of the USSR), Roosevelt (US President) and Churchill (British Prime Minister) – agreed that the Soviet Union could have a **'sphere of influence'** in Eastern Europe.

However, there were differences of opinion over Germany's future:

- Stalin wished to punish and severely weaken Germany with reparations
- Churchill and Roosevelt wanted to rebuild Germany. They remembered the mistakes of the Treaty of Versailles.

The Yalta Conference, February 1945

At the Yalta Conference, the Allied leaders (Churchill, Roosevelt and Stalin) got on well together. The following points were agreed.

- Germany would be divided into four zones. These would be run by the USA, France, Britain and the USSR.
- Germany's capital city, Berlin (which was in the Soviet zone), would also be divided into four zones.
- The countries of eastern Europe would be allowed to hold free elections to decide how they would be governed.
- The USSR would join in the war against Japan in return for territory in Manchuria and Sakhalin Island.

The Potsdam Conference, July–August 1945

In April 1945 President Roosevelt died, so at the Potsdam Conference the USA was represented by a new President, Harry Truman. During the conference, Churchill was replaced by Clement Attlee as British Prime Minister. The new leaders did not get on as well with Stalin as Roosevelt and Churchill had done.

There was agreement on some points.

- The Nazi Party was to be banned and its leaders would be tried as war criminals.
- The Oder–Neisse (two rivers) line was to form part of the border between Poland and Germany.

However, there were disagreements on other issues. There were clear signs that Stalin did not trust the USA and Britain and that they did not trust him.

Tensions at Potsdam

1 Britain and the USA denied Stalin a naval base in the Mediterranean.
- They saw no need for Stalin to have such a base.
- Stalin saw this as evidence that his allies mistrusted him.

Key term

'Sphere of influence': an area under Soviet control, which meant countries in Eastern Europe.

Exam tip Candidates often confuse the key features of these two conferences of 1945. Ensure you know who attended and what was agreed at each conference.

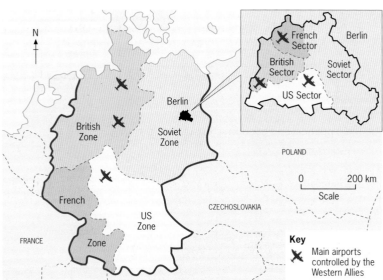

The division of Germany after the war.

Attlee **Truman** **Stalin**

2 Stalin wanted more reparations from Germany than Britain and the USA did.
- The USA and Britain did not wish to cripple Germany; they had seen the results of harsh reparations after the First World War.
- Stalin was suspicious about why his allies seemed to want to protect Germany and even help it recover.

3 Stalin had set up a Communist government in Lublin, the capital of Poland. Britain preferred the non-Communist Polish Government, which had lived in exile in Britain throughout the war. Truman and Attlee were very suspicious of Stalin's motives in setting up a Communist government.

The atom bomb further worsened relations between the USA and USSR during the Potsdam Conference. Stalin had been told about the atom bomb by Truman at the start of the Potsdam Conference and was furious that it had been kept a secret. The use of the atom bomb increased rivalry between the superpowers:
- Stalin was convinced that the USA was using the bombs as a warning to the USSR.
- Truman was convinced that the USA had the ultimate weapon and this made him even more determined to stand up to Stalin and prevent further Soviet expansion.
- An arms race emerged with the USSR determined to develop its own atom bomb.

> ## Exam practice
>
> **1** Describe the key features of the Yalta Conference.
>
> *(6 marks)*

> **Exam tip** This is a question 4 from Unit 1. You will need to give at least two precise developed statements to achieve full marks.

> ## Key term
>
> **Satellite state:** a country under the influence or control of another state.

> ## Revision tasks
>
> **1** Make a copy of the table below and add notes on what was agreed/where there was disagreement.
>
> | Conference | Points agreed | Areas of disagreement |
> |---|---|---|
> | Teheran | | |
> | Yalta | | |
> | Potsdam | | |
>
> **2** What important changes had occurred between the Teheran and the Potsdam Conferences?

1.2 The development of the Cold War, 1945–48

By the end of 1945 it became clear that Europe had been divided between capitalism in the west and Communism in the east. The countries of eastern Europe became Soviet **satellite states**.

Soviet satellite states

The Soviet Red Army advanced through large areas of eastern Europe whilst driving back the Germans. One year after the war, many Soviet troops were still stationed in much of eastern Europe.

Elections were held in each eastern European country, as promised at Yalta in 1945, but the evidence suggests that they were rigged to allow the USSR-backed Communist parties to take control. In Bulgaria, Albania, Poland, Romania and Hungary, opponents of the Communists were beaten, murdered or frightened into submission.

By 1948, all eastern European states had Communist governments.

Key
- — Iron Curtain
- ····· Pre-war USSR boundary
- — Post-war USSR boundary
- ☭ Communist states under USSR control

The spread of Communism, 1945–48.

Europe was now divided – East and West. In 1946, Churchill called this division the 'Iron Curtain'. He said:

> From Stettin on the Baltic to Trieste on the Adriatic, an iron curtain has descended across the Continent. Behind that line lie all the capitals of Central and Eastern Europe … and all are subject to a very high measure of control from Moscow.

Revision tasks

Using the information on page 13 and above, answer the following questions.

1 What is meant by:
   - the 'Iron Curtain'
   - satellite states?

2 Make a copy of the table below and, in no more than one sentence, summarise the views of each side about Soviet expansion in eastern Europe.

Soviet view	
US view	

US involvement in Europe

In 1947 the USA committed itself to a policy of containment of Communism in Europe. Truman had received worrying news in the 'Long Telegram', a secret report from Kennan, America's ambassador in Moscow. The telegram suggested that Stalin was determined to destroy capitalism by building up his military power.

Greece

You can see from the map on page 13 that Greece appeared to be next in line in the spread of Communism. Greek resistance against the Germans had been divided into two movements – the royalists (who wanted the return of the king) and the Communists. After the war, the royalists restored the king with the help of British troops. However, they came under attack from Communist forces and asked the USA for help in early 1947.

Truman was already very worried about the spread of Communism. Under a foreign policy initiative that became known as the Truman **Doctrine**, the USA provided Greece with arms, supplies and money. The Communists were defeated in 1949 after a civil war.

The Truman Doctrine, 1947

Events in Greece convinced Truman that unless he acted, Communism would continue to spread. He therefore explained his policy to the world. This became known as the Truman Doctrine. Truman said:

> I believe it must be the policy of the USA to support all free people who are resisting attempted subjugation by armed minorities or by outside pressure.

- The USA would not return to isolationism – it would play a leading role in the world.
- The aim was to contain (stop the spread of) Communism but not to push it back. This became the policy of **containment**.

Comment

Stalin was simply carrying out his policy of making sure he had friendly governments on his doorstep. However, to the British and Americans, he seemed to be trying to build up a Communist empire.

Exam practice

1 Explain why relations between the USA and the USSR had changed by the end of 1946. *(13 marks)*

You may use the following in your answer:
- the Iron Curtain
- satellite states

You must also include information of your own.

Exam tip The Exam practice question above is an example of a question 6 from Unit 1. You need to:
- use the two factors given in the bullet points, adding good relevant detail
- add one more factor from your own knowledge
- show clearly how each factor led to change in relations between the USA and USSR
- prioritise the reasons. In other words, explain which you think was the most important and why.

Key terms

Doctrine: a statement of ideas.
Containment: a foreign policy aimed at containing the political influence or military power of another country – for example, US policy to stop the spread of Communism during the Cold War.

The Marshall Plan

The USA also became committed to the economic recovery of western Europe to prevent the spread of Communism.

Truman believed that poverty and hardship provided a breeding ground for Communism, so he wanted to make Europe prosperous again. It was also important for American businesses to have trading partners in the future, yet Europe's economies were still in ruins after the war.

The American Secretary of State, George Marshall, therefore visited Europe and came up with a European recovery programme – usually known as the Marshall Plan or **Marshall Aid**. This had two main aims:

- to stop the spread of Communism (Truman did not admit this at the time)
- to help the economies of Europe to recover (this would eventually provide a market for American exports).

Between 12 and 13 billion dollars poured into Europe in the years 1947–51, providing vital help for Europe's economic recovery. However, Marshall Aid also caused tensions:

- Only sixteen European countries accepted it – and these were all western European states.
- Stalin refused Marshall Aid for the USSR and banned eastern European countries from accepting it. Instead, he created his own organisations known as Cominform and Comecon.

The Soviet response

Cominform, 1947

In 1947, Stalin set up Cominform – an alliance of Communist countries – probably as a response to the Marshall Plan. Its aim was to spread Communist ideas, but it also helped Stalin tighten his hold on his Communist allies because it restricted their contact with the West.

Only one Communist leader, Marshall Tito of Yugoslavia, was not prepared to accept Stalin's total leadership. He split with Moscow. However, Yugoslavia remained Communist.

Comecon, 1949

Set up by Stalin to co-ordinate the production and trade of the eastern European countries, it was like an early Communist version of the European Community. However, Comecon favoured the USSR more than any of its other members.

Bizonia

By 1947, the British and American zones were operating as one and became 'Bizonia', meaning two zones. Bizonia and the French zone later became 'Trizonia'.

> ## Comment
>
> *Marshall Aid was a generous gesture by the USA but it was not entirely an act of kindness. Stalin saw it as an attempt by American business to dominate western Europe. If the USA was determined to 'buy' western Europe with its dollars, then he was determined to control eastern Europe with his Communist allies and the Red Army.*

> **Exam tip** Candidates often confuse the Truman Doctrine and the Marshall Plan. Ensure you have a thorough knowledge of both. Remember the Truman Doctrine is about political aid to western Europe to contain the spread of Communism and the Marshall Plan is economic aid.

Revision tasks

1 The Truman Doctrine and the Marshall Plan were described as being two sides of the same coin. Make your own copy of both sides of this imaginary coin, big enough to write in. On one side give a brief definition of the Truman Doctrine. On the other side write a brief definition of the Marshall Plan.

2 How far do you feel each side was to blame for the tension after the Second World War? Decide where you would put the USA and the USSR on the scale below:

Mostly to blame ⟵————————⟶ Not to blame

1.3 The development of the Cold War, 1948–56

The Cold War intensified in the years after 1948 due to the Berlin Crisis of 1948–49, the formation of rival alliance systems and the nuclear arms race.

The Berlin blockade and airlift, 1948–49

This was the first major crisis of the Cold War.

Causes

Germany's economy and government had been shattered by the war and the Allies were faced with a serious question: should they continue to occupy Germany or should they try to rebuild it?

- Britain and the USA wanted Germany to recover – they could not afford to keep feeding its people and they felt that punishing Germany would not help future peace.
- The USSR did not want to rebuild Germany and Stalin was suspicious about why the USA and Britain did.

In 1948, the French, American and British zones merged to become one zone, 'Trizonia' (in August 1949 this area became known as West Germany). With the help of Marshall Aid, West Germany began to recover and prosper. It was a very different story in East Germany. In this area, controlled by the USSR, there was poverty and hunger. Many East Germans were leaving because West Germany seemed a much more attractive place to live.

In Stalin's eyes, it seemed that the Allies were building up West Germany in order to attack him. When in 1948 they introduced a new West German currency (the Deutsche Mark), it was the last straw.

Events

Stalin tried to **blockade** Berlin, the former capital of Germany, in East Germany (see map on page 13). In a month, he closed all road and rail connections from Berlin to West Germany, hoping he could force the western Allies out of the city. For many people at the time, it seemed there was a real risk of war. The USA and Britain faced a choice:

- they could withdraw – but this would be humiliating and it might encourage Stalin to think he could invade West Germany
- they could lift supplies into West Berlin by air – they had the planes but it would be risky as they might be shot down.

The Allies decided to airlift supplies. The airlift lasted until the following Spring of 1949 and reached its peak on 16–17 April when 1,398 flights landed nearly 13,000 tonnes of supplies in 24 hours. During the airlift West Berliners were supplied with everything from food and clothing to oil and building supplies. It was a great success.

Results

By May 1949, the USSR lifted the blockade. It was a victory for the West, but relations with the USSR hit rock bottom. Co-operation in Germany in the future was very unlikely and the country would remain divided. The zone controlled by the USA, Britain and France became the Federal Republic of Germany (West Germany) in August 1949. In October 1949, the Soviet zone became the German Democratic Republic (East Germany).

> ### Revision task
> Draw a flow chart to show the causes, events and results of the Berlin crisis of 1948–49.

Exam practice

SOURCE A

From a school textbook written in 1984, describing the Berlin airlift.

'The Berlin airlift was a considerable achievement but neither side gained anything from the confrontation. The USSR had not gained control of Berlin. The West had no guarantees that land communications would not be cut again. Above all, it made both sides even more stubborn.'

1 Give TWO reasons from Source A which show that the Berlin airlift made both sides in the Cold War 'even more stubborn'. (Lines 14–15.)

(2 marks)

Exam tip The Exam practice question above is an example of a question 1 from Unit 1. You need to write two short sentences based on items from the source explaining why the Berlin airlift made both sides more stubborn.

Key term

Blockade: the surrounding of a place with troops or ships to prevent the entry or exit of supplies.

Exam tip Candidates often confuse this crisis with the crisis over the Berlin Wall in 1961. An easy way to remember the difference is 'B' for blockade comes before 'W' for wall.

Rival alliances

By 1956 there were two rival alliance systems each dominated by one of the superpowers.

NATO (North Atlantic Treaty Organisation), 1949

This military alliance contained most of the states in western Europe as well as the USA and Canada. Its main purpose was to defend its members. If one member was attacked, the other members would help to defend it. When the USSR developed its own atomic bomb in 1949, NATO seemed even more important to the defence of western Europe, since at the time no western European country had atomic weapons.

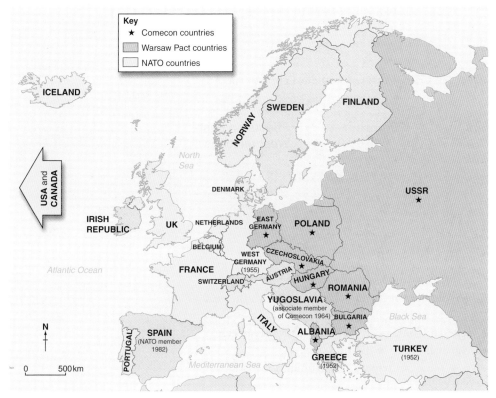

Alliances, 1949–55.

The importance of NATO

- The USA was now formally committed to the defence of western Europe.
- Stalin did not see it as a defensive alliance but as a direct threat to the USSR.
- The USA was able to build air bases in western Europe where planes armed with nuclear weapons could be stationed ready for use against the Soviet Union.

The Warsaw Pact

In 1955, West Germany joined NATO. The Soviet response was to set up the Warsaw Pact – a Communist version of NATO. The Soviets had not forgotten the damage that Germany had inflicted on the USSR in the Second World War.

The nuclear arms race

- During 1945–49, the USA was the only country to possess atomic weapons.
- In 1949, the USSR successfully tested an atomic bomb.
- In 1952, the USA detonated its first hydrogen bomb.
- In 1953, the USSR tested its own hydrogen bomb.

Exam tip Questions on NATO are often not well answered as candidates fail to revise its features and importance. Ensure you revise these thoroughly.

Comment

All of the alliances demonstrated the fear and mistrust that brought about the Cold War. The western democracies and the USSR both feared the rise of another state like Nazi Germany. However, each side saw the other as this potential threat, certainly not itself. The creation of alliances for self-defence on one side could very easily look like an alliance preparing to attack the other side.

By 1953, the USSR appeared to be catching up with the USA in the developing arms race. The balance tilted even more in the direction of the USSR when China became Communist in October 1949. In 1950, Stalin and the new Chinese Communist leader, Mao Zedong, signed a 30-year treaty of friendship.

In 1957, the arms race moved into a new phase with the development of satellites. These meant that nuclear bombs would no longer have to be dropped from long-range aircraft but could be launched out of the Earth's atmosphere and guided towards a target. In 1957, the USSR used a rocket to launch Sputnik I into orbit around the Earth. The Americans developed their own rockets. The 'space race' had begun.

Both countries then developed ICBMs (Inter-Continental Ballistic Missiles), which were long-range missiles that could be launched from underground bases. The USA also created Polaris missiles, which could be fired from a submarine, with a range of over 1,600 kilometres. The USSR developed its own version.

> ## Comment
>
> *The Polaris missile was a Submarine-Launched Ballistic Missile (SLBM) carrying a nuclear warhead developed during the Cold War for the US Navy. It was gradually replaced by the Poseidon missile from 1972 onwards.*

Revision tasks

1 Using the information on pages 16–17 and above, complete a copy of the table below.

Organisation	Members	Purpose	Effects on East–West relations
Marshall Plan			
Comecon			
Cominform			
NATO			
Warsaw Pact			

2 Put the following events of the Cold War in chronological order with the year they took place.
- Setting up of NATO
- Teheran Conference
- 'Iron Curtain' speech
- Potsdam Conference
- Marshall Plan
- Berlin Crisis
- Setting up of Warsaw Pact
- Yalta Conference
- Truman Doctrine

1.4 Hungary: the tightening of control

In 1956, an attempted uprising was brutally crushed by the USSR.

The uprising

Causes

Hungary had been treated as a defeated country by the Soviets after the Second World War and, with the support of the USSR, a Communist government had been established under its leader, Mátyás Rákosi, who closely followed Stalin's rules. The Hungarians hated Rákosi and his secret police (the AVH) because of the brutality they had shown, executing or imprisoning thousands of opponents. There were protests against the falling standard of living and increased poverty, which they blamed on Soviet policies.

Events

The protests got worse and Stalin's statue was pulled down and dragged through the streets. Rákosi was forced to resign and Soviet tanks moved in. Imre Nagy became Prime Minister and the Soviet troops withdrew. Nagy was determined on reform. He wanted free elections, the end of the secret police and the removal of the Soviet army of occupation.

However, Khrushchev became alarmed when Nagy demanded the right for Hungary to withdraw from the Warsaw Pact and follow a neutral role in the Cold War. This was too much for the USSR. Free elections could mean the end of Communism in Hungary. If Hungary withdrew from the Warsaw Pact, there would be a gap in the Iron Curtain; the Soviet buffer zone with the West would be broken.

Soviet troops and 1,000 tanks moved into Hungary to crush the uprising. Nagy appealed to the West for help but none came. Two weeks of fighting followed but the Hungarians were no match for the Soviet forces. Nagy was captured, then shot.

Results

- Between 2,500 and 30,000 Hungarians, mostly civilians, were killed along with 700 Soviet troops. Over 200,000 refugees fled Hungary and settled in the West.
- The uprising highlighted the limitations of Khrushchev's policy of **peaceful co-existence**.
- There was no active support for the uprising in the West. This was because Britain, France and the USA were preoccupied with the Suez Crisis.
- A new pro-Soviet government was set up under János Kádár. Kádár re-established Communist control of Hungary and negotiated the withdrawal of Soviet troops once the crisis was over.
- Other satellite states in eastern Europe did not dare to challenge Soviet authority after the events in Hungary.

Revision tasks

1 Make a copy of the table below and summarise the part played by each person in the Hungarian uprising.

Nagy	
Khrushchev	
Kádár	
Rákosi	

2 Draw a timeline for the years 1945–56. On the timeline:
   a) include the key events of the Cold War
   b) briefly explain how each event worsened relations between the two superpowers.

Key content

You need to have a good working knowledge of the following areas. **Tick off each item** once you are confident in your knowledge:

- ☐ the Teheran, Yalta and Potsdam Conferences
- ☐ the ideological differences between the superpowers and the concept of the 'Iron Curtain'
- ☐ the establishment and control of the Soviet satellite states
- ☐ Cominform and Comecon
- ☐ the Truman Doctrine and the Marshall Plan
- ☐ the causes, events and results of the Berlin crisis of 1948–49
- ☐ NATO and the Warsaw Pact
- ☐ the nuclear arms race
- ☐ the causes, events and results of the Hungarian uprising of 1956.

Check your knowledge online with our Quick quizzes at www.hodderplus.co.uk/modernworldhistory.

Key term

Peaceful co-existence: the policy of co-operation rather than rivalry with the West.

Comment

The Suez crisis was a war fought by Britain, France and Israel against Egypt in October 1956. It followed the decision by President Nasser of Egypt to nationalise the Suez Canal. Both the USA and the USSR objected to the attack on Egypt and forced Britain, France and Israel to withdraw.

Exam practice

1 Outline TWO reasons for the Hungarian uprising of 1956. *(4 marks)*

Exam tip The Exam practice question above is an example of a question 2 from Unit 1. You need to:
- give two reasons for the Hungarian uprising
- give one extra sentence for each, giving relevant details.

Chapter 2: Three Cold War crises: Berlin, Cuba and Czechoslovakia *c.*1957–69

The Cold War intensified in the 1960s with three crises: the Berlin Wall in 1961, the Cuban Missile Crisis in 1962 and Czechoslovakia in 1968.

Key topics

These are the key topics you need to revise. As with all examination topics you first need to learn the content so you know it well enough to answer a range of questions on this topic.

- Berlin: a divided city
- Cuba: the world on the brink of war
- Czechoslovakia: the Prague Spring, 1968.

2.1 Berlin: a divided city

In 1961 the Cold War reached another turning point with the construction of the Berlin Wall.

The situation in Berlin

Berlin had always been a source of conflict between the Soviets and western Allies. In 1958 Khrushchev issued the Berlin Ultimatum, demanding that the west withdraw its forces from West Berlin. Capitalist West Berlin, surrounded by the Communist state of East Germany, continued to be a problem for East Germany and the USSR.

- The high standard of living enjoyed by the people of West Berlin contrasted sharply with the poor living conditions in Communist East Berlin.
- It was estimated that 3 million people had crossed from East to West Berlin between 1946 and 1960. Many of these people were skilled workers and it seemed that the economic survival of East Germany was in doubt if this escape route remained open.

The building of the Wall

In 1961, Khrushchev and the East German leadership decided to act. Without warning, on 13 August 1961, the East Germans began to build a wall surrounding West Berlin.

- At first, the structure was little more than a barbed wire fence, but by 17 August it was replaced with a stone wall.
- All movement between East and West Berlin was stopped.
- For several days, Soviet and American tanks faced each other across divided Berlin streets.

The building of the Berlin Wall had some immediate effects.

- The flow of refugees was reduced to a trickle.
- Western nations won a propaganda victory since it appeared that Communist states needed to build walls to prevent their citizens from leaving.

However, the western nations had to be satisfied with a propaganda victory only. It was clear that the USA and NATO were not going to try to stop the building of the Wall. In reality, there was little the western powers could do to stop it.

Revision task

As you work through chapter 2 use the table on page 24 to guide reading. Make notes as you go along.

Exam practice

1 Describe the key features of the Berlin crisis of 1961.

(6 marks)

Exam tip The Exam practice question above is an example of a question 4 from Unit 1. You need to give good relevant detail of at least two aspects of the event to gain full marks.

Kennedy's response

From the 1960s until the 1980s, the Berlin Wall became a symbol of the division between the capitalist West and the communist East. American President John F. Kennedy made a historic visit to West Berlin in 1963 and declared that the city was a symbol of the struggle between the forces of freedom and the Communist world. For the USSR and East Germany, however, the wall was simply an economic and political necessity. The loss of so many refugees from East Germany had been threatening the very existence of the state.

> **Exam tip** Candidates often confuse this crisis with the crisis over the Berlin blockade in 1948. An easy way to remember the difference is 'B' for blockade comes before 'W' for wall.

> ### Revision tasks
> 1 Why was Khrushchev so determined to force the USA out of West Berlin?
> 2 What were the effects of the construction of the Berlin Wall?

2.2 Cuba: the world on the brink of war

The Cuban missile crisis was the most serious conflict between the USSR and the USA in the history of the Cold War. Cuba was a Communist country just 144 kilometres off the coast of the USA. In October 1962, American spy planes identified nuclear missile sites being built on Cuba.

Castro and Cuba

Cuba had become Communist after a takeover by Fidel Castro in 1958. He was popular in Cuba, in part because he gave land seized from wealthy Americans to the Cuban people.

The USA had retaliated by cutting off aid to Cuba, and refused to buy Castro's cotton and tobacco. In return, Castro secured help from the USSR. Khrushchev was keen to gain influence in Cuba, close to the USA's south-eastern coastline.

In spring 1961, the USA had a new President, John F. Kennedy. He was alarmed at what he saw as a Communist threat on the USA's doorstep. He gave American support to an invasion of Cuba by rebels opposed to Castro's Government. The landing took place at the Bay of Pigs, and was a disaster. There was no popular support for it in Cuba.

> ### Comment
> *In some ways, the Cuban missile crisis was the height of Cold War tension. Never before had the world been so close to nuclear conflict as it was in October 1962. However, the crisis resulted in arms reductions and improved communications (if not better relations) between the USA and the USSR.*

Events of the crisis, 1962

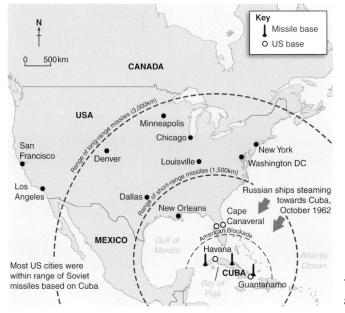

The position and threat of Cuban missiles, and the crisis at its peak, October 1962.

The crisis lasted for thirteen days.

16 October	Kennedy was told that Khrushchev intended to build missile sites in Cuba.	24 October	Khrushchev issued a statement insisting that the Soviet Union would use nuclear weapons in the event of a war.
18–19 October	Kennedy held talks with his closest advisers. The 'Hawks' wanted an aggressive policy whilst the 'Doves' favoured a peaceful solution.	25 October	Kennedy wrote to Khrushchev asking him to withdraw missiles from Cuba.
20 October	Kennedy decided to impose a naval **blockade** around Cuba to prevent Soviet missiles and equipment reaching Cuba. The Americans searched any ship suspected of carrying arms or missiles.	26 October	Khrushchev replied to Kennedy's letter. He said he would withdraw the missiles if the USA promised not to invade Cuba and withdraw its missiles from Turkey.
21 October	Kennedy made a broadcast to the American people, informing them of the potential threat and what he intended to do.	27 October	A US spy plane was shot down over Cuba. Attorney General Robert Kennedy (brother of the President) proposed a deal with the Soviet Union. The USA would withdraw missiles from Turkey as long as it was kept secret.
23 October	Khrushchev sent a letter to Kennedy insisting that Soviet ships would force their way through the blockade.	28 October	Khrushchev accepted the deal.

Results of the crisis

The Cuban crisis had a major effect on East–West relations.
- Leaders of both the USSR and the USA realised that nuclear war had been a real possibility and it was vital that a similar crisis should not happen again.
- The Americans and Soviets decided to set up a telephone link (or 'hot line') so that direct communication could take place in future between Washington and Moscow. Nuclear arms talks also began and, in 1963, a Test Ban Treaty was signed between the USA, the USSR and Britain.

Key term

Blockade: the surrounding of a place with troops or ships to prevent the entry or exit of supplies.

Revision tasks

1 Using the information on page 21 and above, complete a copy of the table below and summarise the part played by each person in the Cuban missile crisis.

Castro	
John Kennedy	
Robert Kennedy	
Khrushchev	

2 Place the following events of the crisis in chronological order.
- an American U-2 plane is shot down over Cuba
- the USA blockade Cuba
- Khrushchev accepts the deal
- the US discover Soviet missile sites on Cuba
- Robert Kennedy suggests a deal.

3 Which country do you think gained the most from the crisis: the USA, the USSR or Cuba? Explain your answer.

Exam tip The Cuban missile crisis is a popular exam topic. Ensure you thoroughly revise the causes, events and results.

2.3 Czechoslovakia: the Prague Spring, 1968

In 1968 the USSR once again showed its unwillingness to allow greater freedom in the Eastern Bloc.

In 1967, Alexander Dubček had become Communist Party Secretary in Czechoslovakia. In the spring of 1968 (the 'Prague Spring'), Dubček began to reform the Communist system.

- Censorship of the press was ended.
- Other political parties apart from the Communist Party were allowed.
- Some political prisoners were released and Czech citizens were given greater freedom to travel abroad.

The reforms in Czechoslovakia became known as 'Communism with a human face'. They seemed to represent the general easing of tension between East and West that had taken place after the Cuban crisis.

Soviet reaction

However, Dubček's reforms were seen as a major threat by the new leader of the USSR, Brezhnev. As in Hungary twelve years earlier, action was taken to prevent the reforms from sweeping the Communists out of power in Czechoslovakia and spreading to the rest of eastern Europe.

- In August 1968, 400,000 Warsaw Pact troops entered Czechoslovakia, arrested leading reformers and seized key towns and cities.
- Dubček and the Czech President Svoboda were flown to Moscow where they talked with Brezhnev for four days.
- On 27 August, the Czech leaders returned and announced that many of their reforms were to be stopped and censorship reintroduced. In 1969 Dubček resigned and was replaced by a loyal Communist, Husak.

Reaction from the rest of the world

America was fighting a bloody war against Communism in Vietnam. It knew that Brezhnev would not interfere in Vietnam if the USA did not intervene in Czechoslovakia. The western European governments followed America's lead. They condemned the invasion but did nothing.

However, the Soviet invasion did lead to discontent in eastern Europe. Yugoslavia and Romania condemned the invasion and formed alliances with China, the other major Communist power and now a rival of the USSR.

The Brezhnev Doctrine

After the failure of the Czechs to gain more freedom from Soviet control, the new Czech leader, Husak, set about returning to the old ways. The reforms of the Prague Spring were reversed, and the USSR was once more firmly in control of Czech policy.

Brezhnev then set out what became known as the Brezhnev Doctrine. He argued that a threat to one socialist (that is, Communist) country was a threat to them all. (This doctrine clearly echoed the Truman Doctrine of 1947 and the American fear of the domino effect.) However, he went on to say that force would be used whenever necessary to keep the Soviet satellites firmly under Soviet influence.

This doctrine and the Soviet actions in Czechoslovakia in 1968 did nothing to improve relations between the USSR and the USA. Yet, in spite of it, there was a thaw in relations very quickly in what has become known as the process of **Détente**.

Exam practice

1 Outline TWO results of the Soviet invasion of Czechoslovakia.
(4 marks)

Exam tip The Exam practice question above is an example of a question 2 from Unit 1. You need to:
- give two results of the Soviet invasion of Czechoslovakia
- give one extra sentence for each, giving relevant details.

Comment

The end of the Prague Spring showed once again that the Soviet leadership would not tolerate reform in its satellite states and that the West was unwilling to risk nuclear war over eastern European countries.

Key term

Détente: the relaxing of tension or hostility between nations – for example, the improvement of relations between the USA and the USSR at the end of the 1960s.

Exam practice

SOURCE B

From a speech by a Czech reformer, March 1968.

'In Czechoslovakia the people who were trusted ... were the obedient ones, those who did not cause any trouble, who didn't ask questions. It was the mediocre man who came off best.'

SOURCE C

From a BBC interview with a Czech reform leader, May 1968.

'Socialism is for us the only possibility. We lived under another system 25 years ago and it was not a happy time for us. The main change we want is just to bring back a human face to socialism, to find a more honest, more human way to fulfil the aims we have in mind.'

1 How useful are Sources B and C as evidence of the reasons for the Prague Spring? Explain your answer using Sources B and C and your own knowledge.   *(10 marks)*

Revision tasks

1 Using the information on page 23 and above, complete a copy of the table below. Write in note form and be concise.

Crises	Causes	Effects
1 Berlin crisis, 1961		
American view		
Soviet view		
2 Cuban missile crisis		
American view		
Soviet view		
3 Czechoslovakia		
American view		
Soviet view		

2 Which of the three crises was the most serious threat to world peace? Give reasons for your decision.

Exam tip   The Exam practice question on the left is an example of a question 3 from Unit 1. You need to judge the usefulness of *both* sources on the basis of:
- what is in the sources, what each one says, how accurate it is
- the nature, origin and purpose of each source: who is speaking, who they were and when they were speaking.

Use this evaluation to compare the **usefulness** of each source in answering the question (explaining the reasons for the Prague Spring).

Exam practice

2 Describe the key features of the Prague Spring.   *(6 marks)*

Exam tip   The Exam practice question above is an example of a question 4 from Unit 1. You need to give good relevant detail of at least two aspects of the event to gain full marks.

Key content

You need to have a good working knowledge of the following areas. **Tick off each item** once you are confident in your knowledge.

- ☐ the reasons for the building of the Berlin Wall, including the refugee problem and the failure of the summit conferences
- ☐ the construction of the Berlin Wall and its effects on East–West relations
- ☐ Kennedy's reaction to the Wall and his visit to Berlin, 1963
- ☐ the causes of the Cuban missile crisis, including Castro and the USSR and the Bay of Pigs
- ☐ the events of the crisis and how it was resolved
- ☐ short- and long-term effects of the missile crisis
- ☐ opposition to Soviet control of Czechoslovakia and the Prague Spring
- ☐ Soviet reactions and the invasion of Czechoslovakia
- ☐ the Brezhnev Doctrine and its effects.

Check your knowledge online with our Quick quizzes at www.hodderplus.co.uk/modernworldhistory.

Chapter 3: Why did the Cold War end? From Détente (1972) to the collapse of the Soviet Union (1991)

25

The final part of the Cold War started with the Russian invasion of Afghanistan and President Reagan's reference to the Soviet Union as 'that evil empire'. Yet within a few years relations were improving. Then, suddenly, at the end of the 1980s the USSR started to lose control of its satellite countries and by 1991 the USSR had disintegrated. The Cold War was over.

Key topics

These are the key topics you need to revise. As with all examination topics you first need to learn the content so you know it well enough to answer a range of questions on this topic.

- the collapse of Détente – the effects of the Soviet invasion of Afghanistan, 1979
- President Reagan and the 'Second Cold War'
- President Gorbachev and the end of the Cold War.

3.1 The collapse of Détente

The 1970s was a decade associated with **Détente**. There was more contact between leaders and a number of international agreements were made on a range of issues. This ended with the Soviet invasion of Afghanistan and was followed by what became known as the second Cold War.

Détente

Détente meant a general easing of tension in relations between the superpowers. The high point of Détente was the Helsinki Conference of 1975.

Strategic Arms Limitation Talks (SALT)

In 1969, the USA and the USSR began negotiations in an effort to control the arms race. The talks lasted for three years and in 1972 **SALT** I was signed. Both sides agreed to keep the number of nuclear weapons and warheads within strict limits. They also agreed to begin further talks to discuss weapons systems not included in SALT I.

Co-operation in space

Throughout the 1960s, the Americans and Soviets had been arch rivals in the 'space race'. Yet in July 1975, three American astronauts and two Soviet cosmonauts docked their Apollo and Soyuz spacecraft together in orbit around the Earth. It was one of the most visible signs of Détente in action and gave a further impetus to superpower co-operation.

The Helsinki Conference, August 1975

In August 1975 at Helsinki in Finland, 35 countries, including the USSR and the USA, signed the Helsinki Agreement. This was a high point for Détente.

> ## Key terms
>
> **Détente:** the relaxing of tension or hostility between nations – for example, the improvement of relations between the USA and the USSR at the end of the 1960s.
>
> **SALT:** Strategic Arms Limitation Talks, which limited the number of nuclear weapons and warheads held by each side.

- The western powers recognised the frontiers of eastern Europe and Soviet influence in that area.
- West Germany officially recognised East Germany.
- The Soviets agreed to buy American grain and to export oil to the West.
- The Soviets agreed to allow greater freedom in the Soviet Union to western journalists, to give 21 days' notice before holding military manoeuvres near to a frontier, and to allow some inspection of human rights.
- All countries agreed to improve human rights throughout the world.

It should be remembered that these resolutions were not always put into force. For example, abuses of human rights continued in the USSR and other countries after 1975.

Revision task

Using the information on page 25 and above, complete a copy of the following table and summarise the key features of Détente.

The meaning of Détente	
SALT	
Co-operation in space	
The Helsinki Conference	

> **Exam tip** Détente is the least well known period of the Cold War. Ensure you know what it means and its key features.

The Soviet invasion of Afghanistan

The 1970s saw improving relations between the superpowers. However, these were damaged once again by the USSR's invasion of Afghanistan in 1979. The Soviets insisted that they had been invited into Afghanistan to restore order, but western nations protested that it was a straightforward invasion that could not be justified. Despite worldwide protests, the invasion and occupation of Afghanistan continued.

Reasons for the invasion

The Soviets invaded Afghanistan for several reasons.
- They were concerned about the Muslim revolution in neighbouring Iran, which could have spread to Afghanistan and Muslim areas inside the USSR.
- The political situation in Afghanistan was very unstable at the end of the 1970s and the Soviets wanted to maintain their influence in the area.
- Afghanistan was close to the Middle East oil reserves of the western powers and the ports of the Indian Ocean. The Soviets wanted to develop their interests in this area.

> **Key term**
>
> **Mujahidin:** Afghan Muslim freedom fighters who fought against the Soviet occupation using guerrilla tactics.

Consequences

Within weeks of the invasion, Soviet troops were being killed by **Mujahidin** rebels who used very effective guerrilla tactics. The USA secretly began to send very large shipments of money, arms and equipment to Pakistan and from there to the Mujahidin. The campaign became a nightmare for the USSR; unwinnable and a severe drain on its finances.

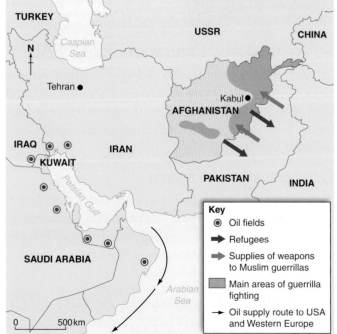

The importance of Afghanistan to the Soviets.

The Carter Doctrine

Following the Soviet invasion, Carter made a statement that became known as the Carter **Doctrine**. The doctrine said that the USA would not allow the USSR to gain control of territory in the oil-rich Middle East.

Carter's actions

President Carter was furious with the Soviet invasion and took action. He pulled the USA out of the 1980 Moscow Olympic Games. (The USSR retaliated in 1984 by pulling out of the Los Angeles Games, see below.) Carter told the Senate not to ratify (agree to) the SALT II treaty that was ready to sign and would have further limited the number of nuclear weapons. He also cut trade between the USA and the USSR – for example, he prevented food and technological goods, such as computers, being sold to the USSR. He also formed an alliance with China and Israel to support the Afghan rebels, providing weapons and funds for the Mujahidin.

Exam tip The Soviet invasion of Afghanistan is one of the most important turning points in the Cold War. It brought an end to Détente and the resumption of the Cold War.

3.2 President Reagan and the 'Second Cold War'

The period following the Soviet invasion of Afghanistan is often described as the Second Cold War.

The 'evil empire'

Ronald Reagan succeeded Carter as President of the USA. He believed that Détente had been a disaster and rejected the idea of **peaceful co-existence** with the USSR. Instead he was determined to get tough and in a speech in 1983 referred to the USSR as 'that evil empire'.

Key terms

Doctrine: a statement of ideas.
Peaceful co-existence: the policy of co-operation rather than rivalry with the West.
Boycott: to refuse to take part in.

'Star Wars'

Reagan was convinced that the USA could win the Cold War. He believed that the USSR should be forced to disarm by his new initiative – SDI (the Strategic Defence Initiative) which was nicknamed 'Star Wars'. It was intended to be a satellite anti-missile system that would orbit the earth to protect the USA from any Soviet missiles. Satellites equipped with powerful lasers would act as a 'nuclear umbrella' against Soviet nuclear weapons.

This was a turning point in the arms race. During détente the two superpowers had been evenly matched. Now the balance was very much in favour of the USA. The USSR could not compete with SDI.

- The Soviet economy could not produce enough wealth to finance the development of new space-based weapons.
- The USSR was well behind the USA in the development of computers, essential for the 'Star Wars' programme.

Exam tip Candidates often lack precise knowledge of the key developments in the Cold War in the years 1979–84. Ensure you revise this section thoroughly.

Revision task

Make a copy of table below. Complete it in note form and be concise.

Development	Key features	Why it worsened relations between the USSR and USA
Soviet invasion of Afghanistan		
'Evil empire' speech		
Strategic Defence Initiative		

The Olympic Games

The Olympic Games of 1980 and 1984 further worsened relations between the two superpowers.

- President Carter led the **boycott** of the 1980 Olympics in Moscow. Sixty countries, including China, Malawi and West Germany, did the same as a sign of protest against the Soviet invasion of Afghanistan.
- The Soviet Union and fourteen other Communist countries retaliated four years later by refusing to take part in the Los Angeles Olympics. The USSR organised the Friendship Games as a Communist alternative.

3.3 President Gorbachev and the end of the Cold War

In March 1985, Mikhail Gorbachev became leader of the Soviet Union and immediately set about reforming the old Soviet system and improving relations with the USA.

Internal reforms

Gorbachev was the decisive figure in this period. He firmly believed that the USSR could not continue to compete with the USA and that the Soviet Union needed to be reformed. The twin themes of his policies were:

- *Perestroika* – changing some economic policies to allow more competition and more incentives to produce goods. Gorbachev wanted to change the government-controlled economy that had been in place since the time of Stalin.
- *Glasnost* – openness in government. Gorbachev thought people should be allowed, within reason, to say what they believe with more open debate.

Ending the Cold War

Gorbachev was able to improve relations with the USA and end the Cold War.

Weaknesses of the USSR

Gorbachev realised that the Soviet Union could not continue the Cold War.

- It was committed to an expensive war in Afghanistan.
- The economy could not sustain increased defence spending.
- The USA seemed to have forged ahead in space and computer technology.
- The USA had also forged ahead in the arms race with the development of SDI.
- There was growing discontent in the satellite states of eastern Europe against Communism and Soviet control. One example of this was the Solidarity trade union movement in Poland which achieved much support in the early 1980s.

Gorbachev and Reagan

The two leaders met on several occasions and got on well together.

- Gorbachev accepted Reagan's invitation to meet with him in Geneva in November 1985. The two leaders were able to talk face-to-face although there was no formal agreement on arms limitations.
- The two met again at Reykjavik in October 1986. Again there was no formal agreement because Reagan refused to drop the SDI project.
- SALT had developed into START (Strategic Arms Reduction Talks) and, on an official visit to Washington in December 1988, Gorbachev also proposed deep cuts in conventional (non-nuclear) American and Soviet forces.

Exam practice

1 Explain why relations between the USA and the USSR changed 1979–85.

You may use the following in your answer:
- Soviet invasion of Afghanistan
- 'evil empire' speech.

You must also include information of your own. *(13 marks)*

Exam tip The Exam practice question above is an example of a question 6 from Unit 1. You need to:
- use the two factors given in the bullet points, adding good relevant detail
- add one more factor from your own knowledge
- show clearly how each factor led to change in relations between the USA and USSR
- link, or prioritise the reasons. In other words, explain which you think was the most important and why.

Comment

These new policies perestroika and glasnost led to many practical changes within the USSR. Some political prisoners were released – for example, Andrei Sakharov, a nuclear physicist-turned-human rights campaigner, was allowed to return from exile. In 1987, changes in economic policy meant that people were allowed to buy and sell at a profit for the first time since the 1920s.

INF treaty

In 1987, after several meetings, Gorbachev and Reagan signed the Intermediate-range Nuclear Forces (INF) treaty, which removed all medium-range nuclear weapons from Europe. Gorbachev signed the treaty because:

- he believed that this would increase his popularity in the West
- the Soviet economy could not recover due to the amount being spent on nuclear weapons
- Reagan told Gorbachev that he had no intention of invading the USSR.

The break-up of eastern Europe

During 1989, Gorbachev was at the height of his international popularity. He met the new American president, George Bush, and together they announced the end of the Cold War. In 1990, he was awarded the Nobel Peace Prize. Yet in 1989, Soviet control of eastern Europe was collapsing rapidly.

The eastern bloc

The Communist countries of eastern Europe had become increasingly discontented during the 1980s. It gradually became clear that the Soviet Union had neither the will nor the power to put down demonstrations or prevent changes in these nations' systems of government. Even so, the speed of the collapse of Soviet control amazed everyone.

- Poland: free elections were held in June 1989. Lech Walesa became the first non-Communist leader in eastern Europe since 1945.
- East Germany: the unpopular East German leader, Erich Honecker, tried to prevent change, but his troops refused to fire on the demonstrators. In November 1989 the Berlin Wall was pulled down.
- Czechoslovakia: in November 1989 there were huge anti-Communist demonstrations. Vaclav Havel, a popular playwright, became the new leader of the country, with free elections in 1990.
- Romania: in a short and bloody revolution in December 1989 the unpopular Communist dictator Nicolae Ceaușescu and his wife Elena were shot.
- Bulgaria: the Communist leader resigned in November 1989 and free elections were held in 1990.
- The Baltic states: in 1990 Lithuania, Latvia and Estonia declared themselves independent of the Soviet Union.

The collapse of Communism in eastern Europe, 1989–1991.

The fall of the Berlin Wall

The fall of the Berlin Wall came to symbolise the end of the Cold War. On 9 November 1989 the East German Government announced much greater freedom of travel for East German citizens, including crossing the border into West Germany. Thousands of East Berliners flocked to the checkpoints in the Berlin Wall and the border guards let them pass. Soon, the East Berliners were chipping away at and dismantling the wall.

The fall of the Soviet Union

Gorbachev was seen as weak by many within the Soviet Union. His promised reforms had not brought about improved living standards and he appeared to have simply allowed the collapse of Soviet influence in eastern Europe. Some in the USSR itself did not want the mere reform of Communism, but its abolition.

In 1991, East and West Berlin were reunited, and East and West Germany became a single country. In other ex-Communist countries there were less happy endings. For example, in Yugoslavia the Serbs refused to accept a Croat as leader, and Slovenia and Croatia declared independence in 1991, leading to a bloody civil war. The era of Communism in eastern Europe was over.

Revision tasks

Using the information on pages 28–29 and above, answer the following questions.

1 Draw a mind map to explain briefly the part played by the following in the collapse of the USSR:
- *Perestroika*
- *Glasnost*
- Boris Yeltsin
- Gorbachev

2 Explain why Gorbachev was so liked and so hated at the same time.

3 Make a copy of the table below and summarise the key developments in each country in the years 1989–90.

Poland	
Czechoslovakia	
East Germany	
Romania	
Bulgaria	
Hungary	
The Baltic states	

Exam practice

1 Explain the importance of THREE of the following in the collapse of the USSR:
- Gorbachev
- *Glasnost*
- *Perestroika*
- Boris Yeltsin.

(15 marks – 5 marks for each part of your chosen three)

Exam tip The Exam practice question above is an example of a question 5 from Unit 1. You need to choose three items and for each one:
- describe it in good detail
- explain clearly why it was important in the collapse of the USSR.

Key content

You need to have a good working knowledge of the following areas.
Tick off each item once you are confident in your knowledge.

- ☐ the meaning of Détente and its key features
- ☐ the reasons for and impact of the Soviet invasion of Afghanistan
- ☐ the reaction of President Carter
- ☐ the Second Cold War, the 'evil empire' and SDI
- ☐ the policies of President Gorbachev
- ☐ the end of the Cold War, including the summits between Reagan and Gorbachev and the INF Treaty
- ☐ the break-up of eastern Europe, including the fall of the Berlin Wall
- ☐ the break-up of the Soviet Union and the fall of Gorbachev.

Check your knowledge online with our Quick quizzes at www.hodderplus.co.uk/modernworldhistory.

In 1918 Germany was defeated in the First World War. The country was in chaos and there were attempts at revolution. In the 1920s Germany recovered, but the Depression caused enormous problems which allowed Hitler and the Nazi Party to gain power. Hitler's Third Reich brought benefits to certain groups in Germany in the period 1933 to 1939, but proved disastrous for others.

Key topics

These are the key topics you need to revise. As with all examination topics you first need to learn the content so you know it well enough to answer a range of questions on this topic.

- the Weimar Republic, 1918–33
- Hitler and the rise of the Nazi Party, 1918–33
- the Nazi dictatorship, 1933–39
- Nazi domestic policies, 1933–39.

4.1 The Weimar Republic, 1918–33

The **Weimar Republic**, which was set up after the First World War, faced a number of problems in its early years. It experienced a period of recovery in the years 1924–29, only to be badly affected by the Great Depression.

The origins of the Weimar Republic, 1918–23

Defeat in the First World War led to the **abdication** of **Kaiser** Wilhelm II and the establishment of a new republic.

There was revolution in Germany in October–November 1918 due to the effects of the First World War:

- The British navy had imposed a naval blockade of German ports which left Germany short of food and essential supplies. The winter of 1917–18 was nicknamed the 'turnip winter' because of the dependence on turnips as a source of food.
- The British, French and US armies had driven the German troops out of France and Belgium and were close to the German borders.
- A flu epidemic was sweeping the country, killing thousands of people already weakened by rations.

The revolution began with sailors in the port of Kiel who, at the end of October 1918, refused to go to sea and instead marched on Berlin. This triggered other revolts. On 9 November the Kaiser abdicated and on the following day a republic was set up under **Chancellor** Ebert. On 11 November the new republic signed the **armistice** with the Allies.

The early problems of the Weimar Republic, 1919–23

Ebert and his colleagues drew up a new democratic **constitution** for Germany and, in the summer of 1919, Ebert was elected its first President.

Key terms

Weimar Republic: a republic is a country without a hereditary ruler, such as a king or emperor. The new Government first met in the town of Weimar.

Abdication: to give up the throne.

Kaiser: emperor.

Chancellor: chief minister (equivalent of Prime Minister in Britain).

Armistice: a ceasefire.

Constitution: an agreed method of governing a country, with the details usually written down and agreed on by those being governed.

A democratic Germany

In theory, the new Weimar constitution gave Germany a nearly perfect democratic system.

- The 'lower house', or Reichstag, was elected by **proportional representation**. The vote was by secret ballot and universal suffrage (everyone could vote). Elections were to be held at least every four years.
- The 'upper house', or Reichsrat, was made up of representatives from each of the German states. It could delay new laws.
- The President was also the head of state and was elected every seven years. The President appointed the Chancellor (usually the head of the largest party in the Reichstag) to form a government. The Chancellor's role was therefore similar to the Prime Minister's role in Britain.

In practice, it proved very difficult to get one party into power (see below).

Weaknesses of the new constitution

- In 1919, the Republic had many enemies. Was it sensible to give equal rights to those who wished to destroy it?
- Proportional representation encouraged lots of small parties. It was difficult for one party to get a majority so governments had to be **coalitions** where two or more parties joined together. This led to weak governments.
- The President had too much power. Article 48 of the constitution said that in an emergency, the President could abandon democracy and rule by decree. This proved disastrous in the period 1929–33.
- The army generals were the same men who had fought the war for the Kaiser. Many of them opposed the Republic and wanted the Kaiser to return.
- The judges in the new Germany were the same men who had served under the Kaiser. They had sympathy with those who were against the Republic.

Effects of the Treaty of Versailles

The German Government had no choice but to sign the treaty, but this had several unfortunate results.

- The new Republic got off to a bad start and was immediately associated with the humiliating treaty.
- Opponents of the Republic, especially the army, blamed the Government for signing the armistice that led to the treaty. They referred to the Government as the 'November Criminals'; a reference to the signing of the armistice on 11 November.
- The Government was accused of having stabbed the German army in the back. In other words, the German army would have won the war if the armistice had not been signed. This, of course, was not true.
- Germany could not afford to pay the reparations. The country had been run down by the war and had lost important areas of land which could make money, such as the coalfields of the Saar.

Key terms

Proportional representation: a system in which the number of representatives from a given party is determined by how many votes that party gains nationally.
Coalition: the joining together of two or more political parties in a situation where no one political party gets a majority of the votes, in order to have sufficient support to pass laws.

Exam tip You will need to know the weaknesses of the German constitution, especially the effects of proportional representation and Article 48.

Exam tip Be aware of the terms of the Treaty of Versailles, how they affected Germany and why they brought widespread opposition.

Exam practice

1 Describe the events which led to the setting up of the Weimar Republic.
(6 marks)

Exam tip The Exam practice question above is an example of a question 1b from Unit 2. You need to give at least two well detailed statements.

Revision tasks

1 Using the information on page 31 and above, draw up a balance sheet of strengths and weaknesses of the new Weimar constitution by writing key words in a table like this:

Strengths	Weaknesses

2 Make a copy of the table below. Complete it to show reasons for German discontent with the Treaty of Versailles.

Military terms	
War guilt	
Rhineland	
Reparations	
Loss of land	

Opposition from the left – the Spartacists

Communists in Germany, known as Spartacists, wanted a revolution similar to that in Russia in 1917 (see page 49).

- In January 1919, Communist activists led by Karl Liebknecht and Rosa Luxemburg seized power in Berlin and the Baltic ports.
- In Bavaria, an independent socialist state was created under the leadership of Kurt Eisner.
- Within weeks, however, all the revolts had been crushed by regular troops and ex-soldiers (Freikorps). The Communist leaders were assassinated.

Opposition from the right – the Kapp Putsch

German **nationalists** thought democracy was weak. For many nationalists, the new Weimar Republic was a symbol of Germany's defeat in the war. They were furious with the Government for signing the Treaty of Versailles. They wanted to see a strong government that would make Germany great once again.

- In March 1920, Wolfgang Kapp, an extreme nationalist, and a group of Freikorps units seized power in Berlin. This became known as the Kapp **Putsch**.
- Kapp was not supported by the workers in the factories. The workers organised a strike in Berlin in support of the Government. Within hours, the German capital came to a halt and supplies of gas, water and coal stopped.
- After four days, Kapp and his supporters gave up and fled Berlin. Ebert and the Weimar Government returned to power.

> ### Key terms
>
> **Nationalists:** those wanting a strong unified Germany, with a government that was similar to the one under the Kaiser before the war.
>
> **Putsch:** an attempt to seize control and gain power by force.

The French occupation of the Ruhr

According to the terms of the Treaty of Versailles, Germany had to pay for the damage caused during the First World War. These payments were known as reparations and were a major burden to the new state.

- The Reparations Commission announced that Germany would be required to pay £6,600 million in gold in annual instalments.
- In 1922, the German Government announced it would not be able to pay and asked for more time.

The British Government agreed to this but the French Government insisted that Germany must pay. In January 1923, the French and Belgian Governments sent troops into the Ruhr, the centre of German industry. The results were disastrous for Germany.

- German workers used **passive resistance** against the invaders and refused to work.
- The German economy ground to a halt.

> ### Key term
>
> **Passive resistance:** a form of opposition in which people do not fight but refuse to co-operate.

Hyperinflation

The problem of making the reparation payments encouraged the Weimar Government to print more and more money. However, printing money simply caused prices to rise out of control and hyperinflation set in. The German mark became virtually worthless.

Value of the German mark against the US dollar, 1914–23	
1914	$1 = 4 marks
1922	$1 = 7,000 marks
July 1923	$1 = 160,000 marks
November 1923	$1 = 4,200,000,000 marks

- As prices rose, people's savings became worthless (this hit the middle classes particularly hard). In 1923, prices in shops were increased almost every hour.
- At times, workers were paid twice a day so that they might be able to buy food before prices rose again.
- People on fixed incomes (such as pensioners) suffered badly.
- Prices rose much faster than incomes and many people starved as they were unable to afford food or fuel.

Revision tasks

1 Make a copy of the table below. Use the information on page 33 and above to write a key word summary of each event and give each a rating on a scale of 1 to 10 in terms of its seriousness for the Weimar Republic.

Threat	Date	Outline of events	Rating
Spartacist revolt			
Kapp Putsch			
French invasion of the Ruhr			
Hyperinflation			

2 Who or what were the following?
   - Spartacists   • Kapp   • Article 48   • the Rentenmark

Exam practice

1 Explain why the Weimar Republic faced attacks from the left and right in the years 1919–23.

(8 marks)

Exam tip The Exam practice question above is an example of a question 1d from Unit 2. You need to:
- fully explain at least two reasons
- show clearly how each led to attacks on the Weimar Republic
- link, or prioritise the reasons. Which do you think was the most important reason and why?

The recovery of the Republic under Stresemann, 1924–29

The role of Stresemann

As Chancellor, Stresemann tried to stabilise Germany's financial position, as shown in the previous section. Stresemann became Foreign Secretary in 1924 and was mainly responsible for the Dawes Plan and German success abroad. He died in October 1929, on the eve of the Wall Street Crash. He was one of the few Weimar politicians strong enough to appeal to the German people.

Economic recovery

This was encouraged by the introduction of:
- the Rentenmark, which replaced the old worthless mark
- the Dawes Plan of 1924 – in return for Germany starting to pay reparations once more, the USA agreed to lend Germany 800 million marks. This could be used to build new factories to produce jobs and goods, and to raise people's standard of living.

During this period, the Weimar Republic seemed to recover from the problems of its early years. This is often referred to as the 'Golden Age' of the Republic. The success was due to several reasons.

- In 1925, the French and Belgian troops left the Ruhr.
- In 1928, industrial production finally improved on pre-First World War levels. By 1930, Germany was one of the leading exporters of manufactured goods.
- In 1929, the Young Plan was introduced, which reduced reparations by over 67 per cent.
- In nearly every town, new factories and public facilities sprang up. New roads, railways, and nearly three million homes were built.

Political stability

The period 1924–29 saw more stable governments. After the 1928 election, the Social Democrats, for the first time since 1923, joined a government coalition with the other parties that supported the Republic. This showed that the middle-class parties were no longer so suspicious of the socialists. There was less support for extreme parties such as the National Socialist German Workers' Party (the Nazis), who won only twelve seats in the Reichstag in the elections of 1928. The Communists also did less well in 1924 and 1928.

Foreign policy

Stresemann was responsible for several successes in foreign policy.

- In 1925 Germany signed the Locarno Treaties with Britain, France and Italy. These guaranteed Germany's frontiers with France and Belgium.
- In 1926 Stresemann took Germany into the League of Nations. Germany was recognised as a great power and was given a permanent seat on the League's Council alongside France and Britain.
- In 1928 Germany signed the Kellogg–Briand Pact along with 64 other nations. It was agreed that they would keep their armies for self-defence but 'the solution of all disputes shall only be sought by peaceful means'.

Problems

However, there were still serious problems.

- Germany depended on American loans, which could be withdrawn at any time.
- Farming suffered from depression throughout the 1920s due to a fall in food prices. Income from agriculture went down from 1925 to 1929.
- Extremist parties such as the Nazis and the Communists were determined to overthrow the Weimar Republic. In 1924 the Communists held 45 seats in the Reichstag and this grew to 54 seats in the 1928 election.
- In 1925 Hindenburg was elected President. He had been one of Germany's war leaders under the Kaiser and disliked the new Republic.

The impact of the Great Depression, 1929–33

The period of recovery under Stresemann ended in 1929 with the Wall Street Crash.

Effects of the Wall Street Crash, 1929

The recovery of the German economy was fragile. It depended heavily on American loans. In 1929, disaster struck with the Wall Street Crash.

- Many American banks were forced to recall their loans. German companies were unable to pay.
- German businesses began to close. Millions lost their jobs.

Unemployment and the rise of extremism

From 1928 to 1930, German unemployment rose from 2.5 million to 4 million. This was an opportunity for extremist groups such as the Communists and the Nazis.

- As unemployment rose, more and more people felt let down by the Weimar Government and began to support extremist parties.
- In the 1930 election, the Communists increased their number of seats in the Reichstag from 54 to 77.
- Nazi support increased from 12 seats in 1928 to 107 in 1930. The Nazis were now the second largest political party in the Reichstag.

Revision tasks

Using the information on pages 34–35 and above, answer the following questions.
1 How had Germany changed in the years 1923–29 as a result of Stresemann's policies? Use a key word list to summarise the changes in the table below.

	1923	1929
The economy		
Political situation		
Foreign policy		

2 Draw a timeline of the Weimar Republic from 1919–30. On your timeline:
   a) add the key developments
   b) shade in red those developments which weakened or threatened the Republic
   c) shade in green those which strengthened it.

4.2 Hitler and the rise of the Nazi Party, 1918–33

The Nazi Party, which was one of the most important extremist groups, was able to take advantage of the problems experienced by the Weimar Republic in the years 1929–32.

The early Nazi Party

Hitler's career before 1919

Hitler was born in Austria in 1889. At the age of sixteen he left school and went to Vienna to pursue his ambition of becoming a painter. This did not work out and between 1909 and 1914 he was virtually destitute, living on the streets of Vienna. It was during these years that he developed his hatred of the Jews:

- **Anti-Semitism** was widespread in Vienna.
- He was envious of the wealthy Jews and blamed them for his own problems.

When war broke out in 1914 Hitler joined the German army and served with distinction, winning the Iron Cross. He found it hard to accept the armistice, believing Germany was on the verge of winning the war when it was betrayed by the politicians. Hitler stayed in the army after the war, working in Munich for the intelligence services. It was in this job that he came across the German Workers' Party led by Anton Drexler.

The Nazi Party, 1919–23

In 1919, Hitler joined the German Workers' Party.
- He changed its name to the National Socialist German Workers' Party (Nazis) and took over as leader in 1921.

> **Key term**
>
> **Anti-Semitism:** hatred of Jews.

> **Exam tip** You will need to be aware of how Hitler's early career shaped his views of the Jews and the Weimar Republic and led him to a career in politics.

- He organised his own private army called the Sturm Abteilung (SA), or Stormtroopers, who were used to protect Nazi meetings and attack those of their opponents, especially the Communists.
- Hitler drew up a 25-point programme, which included the promise to reverse the terms of the Treaty of Versailles, destroy Communism and make Germany great. It also included an attack on the Jews, blaming them for Germany's defeat in the First World War.
- He attracted support from extreme nationalists and by 1922 the Nazi Party had 3,000 members.

The Munich Putsch and the lean years

In 1923 Hitler made his first attempt to seize power.

The Munich Putsch, 1923

In November 1923, Hitler and the Nazis tried to seize control of the Bavarian Government. The plan was to capture Munich and from there march on Berlin. Hitler was convinced people would join him in overthrowing the failed Weimar regime.

Hitler had several reasons for carrying out the Putsch:
- The Weimar Republic was very unpopular due to the French occupation of the Ruhr and hyperinflation.
- In 1922 the Italian leader, Benito Mussolini, had seized power after a march on Rome.
- Hitler was convinced that he would get popular support in Munich.

The attempt is sometimes called the Beer Hall Putsch because of where it began.
- On 8 November, Hitler forced members of the Bavarian Government to join him, at gunpoint. Its leader, Gustav Von Kahr, was reluctant to do so and alerted the army and the police.
- The Nazi plan soon began to go wrong. The next day, Bavarian police opened fire on Nazi Stormtroopers in Munich and sixteen Nazis were killed.
- Hitler and Ludendorff (the former First World War general who was now a Nazi supporter) were arrested and charged with high treason.

However, it was clear that Hitler's views had some support in Germany.
- Hitler received the minimum sentence. Many Nazi supporters also received light sentences.
- Hitler served his sentence in the comfortable Landsberg Fortress and spent his time writing his memoirs.
- The memoirs were later published as *Mein Kampf* (*My Struggle*). In this book, Hitler outlined his view of German history and his views on Germany's rightful place in the world.

Exam practice

1 Explain the effects of the Munich Putsch on Hitler and the Nazi Party. *(8 marks)*

Exam tip The Exam practice question above is an example of a question 1c from Unit 2. You need to give at least two statements which explain the effects of the Munich Putsch. You need to link each effect back to the Putsch, not just describe it.

Revision tasks

1 How did Hitler change the Nazi Party in the period 1919–23?

2 Make a copy of the table below. Use key words to explain the causes, events and results of the Munich Putsch.

	The Munich Putsch
Causes	
Events	
Results	

The lean years, 1924–29

This was a period of mixed fortunes for the Nazi Party. On the one hand, the Nazi Party did not do well.

- It won only twelve seats in the election of 1928.
- There were quarrels and disagreements within the party during Hitler's period in prison.

On the other hand, there was progress.

- Hitler had learnt from the mistake of the Munich Putsch and was determined to achieve power through legal methods – by securing a majority of seats in the Reichstag.
- He reorganised the party to make it more efficient, setting up a headquarters in Munich and branches of the party all over Germany.

Increased support, 1929–33

The Great Depression of 1929 onwards transformed the fortunes of the Nazi Party.

How the Depression helped Hitler

The Depression helped Hitler in several ways.

- It caused a period of chaos in Germany.
- No government could take control of the situation and solve Germany's terrible economic problems.
- Unemployment was the big issue. By January 1932, it stood at 6 million. Hitler promised to get these people back to work. Through clever campaigning and his brilliant speaking skills, Hitler gained support in many parts of German society, including that of wealthy and powerful industrialists. Josef Goebbels was responsible for the Nazi propaganda and election campaigns. He realised the attraction of Hitler's speeches and used air travel to move Hitler quickly from place to place.
- There were frequent street battles between the Communists (Hitler's greatest rivals) and the police. In contrast, the SA gave an impression of discipline and order. Many people felt that the country needed this type of order.

In two years, Hitler led the Nazi Party from being the second largest party in the Reichstag to being the only legal party in Germany. By July 1933, the Weimar Republic and the democracy it represented had been destroyed.

The events of 1932–January 1933

In July 1932 there was a general election which triggered great violence. Nazis and Communists fought each other in street battles and nearly 100 people were killed.

The Nazis became the largest party in the Reichstag and Hitler demanded to be made Chancellor. However, Hindenburg was suspicious of Hitler and refused. Instead, he appointed Franz von Papen, a conservative politician with no party base, as Chancellor.

To achieve his aims, von Papen needed to increase his support in the Reichstag and so he called another election in November 1932. The Nazis lost seats but were still the largest party. Von Papen did not get the extra support he needed.

It was becoming increasingly clear that President Hindenburg could not continue to work with a Chancellor who did not have support in the Reichstag. Von Papen simply could not pass any of the measures he wanted.

In December 1932 Hindenburg replaced von Papen with Kurt von Schleicher, one of his advisers. Within a month, however, von Schleicher was forced to resign.

- Hindenburg and von Papen decided to make Hitler Chancellor.
- They believed they would be able to control him once he was in power.
- On 30 January 1933, Hitler became German Chancellor and von Papen became Vice-Chancellor.

Revision tasks

3 Make a copy of this set of scales. Write in the pans key words about the development of the Nazi Party, 1923–29, including the effects of the Munich Putsch.

4 Do you think the Nazi Party was stronger or weaker in 1929, compared to 1923?

Weaker   Stronger

Exam tip The events of 1932 are very complex. You will need a thorough knowledge of what took place, especially the roles of Hindenburg and von Papen.

Revision tasks

1 What factors changed the prospects for the Nazis between the beginning and end of the 1920s? Use four to six key words for your answer.

2 Draw a flow chart to show the key events of 1932–33 which brought Hitler to power.

3 Do you think that President Hindenburg underestimated Hitler?

4 Put the following events in chronological order:
- the Munich Putsch
- Hitler joins the German Workers' Party
- Hitler is invited to become Chancellor
- the Nazis become the largest party in the Reichstag
- Hitler is in prison
- Hitler introduces the 25-point programme

Exam practice

1 Was the Depression the main reason why Hitler became Chancellor of Germany? You may use the following in your answer:
- the economic Depression
- violence in the streets.

You must also include information of your own. *(16 marks)*

Exam tip The Exam practice question above is an example of a question 3a or 3b from Unit 2. You need to:
- describe in detail the way the Depression helped Hitler to become chancellor using the two bullet-point items you have been given
- add at least one other reason from your own knowledge why he came to power and describe it in detail
- make links between the reasons, or prioritise which you think was the most important and why.

4.3 The Nazi dictatorship, 1933–39

In the years 1933–39 Hitler established a dictatorship of the Nazi Party.

The removal of opposition, 1933–34

As soon as he was appointed Chancellor, Hitler tried to find a way of raising the number of Nazis in his government. He persuaded Hindenburg to dissolve the Reichstag and to hold another general election.

The Reichstag fire, February 1933

During the election campaign, on the night of 27 February 1933, the Reichstag was burnt to the ground. A Communist, Marinus van der Lubbe, was arrested for the crime. Hitler and the Nazis were able to exploit the fire for their own purposes.
- The Nazis were quick to blame the Communist Party.
- Hitler persuaded President Hindenburg to pass an emergency law restricting personal liberty.
- Using the law, thousands of Communist supporters were thrown into prison.

Despite increasing their share of the vote in the election, the Nazis still did not have an overall majority in the Reichstag. They were forced to join together with the 52 nationalist members to create a government.

The Enabling Act, March 1933

Hitler still did not have enough support to have complete control of Germany. An Enabling Act would give him the right to pass laws for the next four years without having to obtain the support of members in the Reichstag. However, to pass an Enabling Act Hitler needed to obtain the votes of two-thirds of Reichstag members, but he had the support of only just over half. This is what happened.
- Hitler ordered his SA to continue intimidating the opposition.
- The 81 Communist members of the Reichstag were expelled.
- In an atmosphere heavy with violence and threats, the Enabling Act was passed by 441 votes to 94.
- Hitler was given the power to rule for four years without consulting the Reichstag.

In July 1933, Hitler increased his grip on power even further. Using the powers of the Enabling Act, he outlawed all other parties and Germany became a one-party state. The democratic Weimar Republic had been destroyed and Germany had become a dictatorship.

Then Hitler turned on the trade unions.

- On 2 May 1933, Nazis broke into trade union offices all over the country and arrested thousands of trade union officials.
- Unions were banned and all workers became part of the German Labour Front.

The Night of the Long Knives

Once he had gained power, Hitler's priority was to rid himself of possible rivals. Ernst Röhm, leader of the SA, had played a major role in helping Hitler achieve power. However:

- The German army saw the SA as a rival – the army would not support Hitler unless the SA was disbanded.
- Some members of the SA looked to Hitler to follow a socialist programme of reform – Hitler was opposed to this since he knew he would lose the support of wealthy industrialists.
- Röhm was a threat to Hitler's dominance of the Nazi Party.

Hitler made a deal with the generals of the German army. They promised to support him as commander-in-chief of the armed forces if the SA was disbanded, and if he started a programme of rearmament. On 30 June 1934, SS assassination squads murdered Hitler's potential SA rivals, including Röhm (the SS was set up in 1925 as an elite section of the SA). It has been estimated that up to 400 people were killed in the 'Night of the Long Knives'.

Just over one month later, President Hindenburg died. Hitler thereafter combined the posts of Chancellor and President and also became commander-in-chief of the armed forces. From this point onwards, soldiers swore personal allegiance to Hitler, who officially became known as *der Führer* (the leader).

Revision task

Using the information on page 39 and above, complete a copy of the table below. Use key words to complete each column to show how Hitler achieved his dictatorship.

	What Hitler did	Importance
Reichstag fire		
The Enabling Act		
The SA		

The police state

In July 1933, Germany became a one-party state. All other political parties were banned and people who openly criticised the Nazis were imprisoned – or worse. This policy was enforced ruthlessly by the SS (Hitler's bodyguard) and the Gestapo (secret police).

- They used terror tactics to intimidate, arrest and even kill any possible opponents.
- Enemies of the Nazis, such as liberals, socialists and Communists, were often arrested and sent to concentration camps without trial.

Exam practice

1 Describe the key features of the police state under the Nazis.

(6 marks)

Exam tip The Exam practice question above is an example of a question 1b from Unit 2. You need to give at least two well detailed statements.

Nazi control of society

The Nazis took control of key areas of everyday life.

Law courts

The legal system was controlled by the Nazis.
- There was no trial by jury.
- All judges were Nazis.

The Churches

The Catholic and Protestant Churches were seen as a threat because Christianity was very different from the beliefs of Nazism.
- A Nazi Reich Church was set up to replace the Protestant Church.
- The Catholic Church was persecuted and priests were arrested.

Censorship and propaganda

The Nazis believed in complete loyalty and obedience. One of the main tools used to achieve this was propaganda. Hitler made Josef Goebbels Minister of Enlightenment and Propaganda. Goebbels' job was to spread Nazi ideas and encourage all Germans to be loyal to Hitler. Goebbels (a former journalist) used his new power to control all information that reached the German people.
- All newspapers were censored by the Government and allowed to print only stories favourable to the Nazis.
- Radio was controlled by the Government. Cheap radios were manufactured so that most Germans could afford one. Goebbels made sure that all radio plays, stories and news items were favourable to the Nazis.
- The Nazis took control of the German film industry. German films of the 1930s often showed great German heroes defeating their enemies. Cartoons were used to show Jews as weak and devious.
- Goebbels organised mass rallies. The most spectacular was held each August in Nuremberg. At the rallies, hundreds of thousands of Nazi supporters listened to choirs, sang songs and watched sporting events and firework displays.
- The Nazis used sporting events to spread their propaganda. The 1936 Berlin Olympic Games was used by the Nazis to suggest the superiority of the 'Aryan race'. ('Aryan' was the Nazi term for non-Jewish Germans.)

> **Exam tip** Remember that Nazi control was based on fear, through the police state, and persuasion, through censorship and propaganda.

> **Revision task**
>
> Draw a mind map to show all the different methods used by the Nazis to control the German people – this should include the police state, censorship and propaganda.

4.4 Nazi domestic policies, 1933–39

Nazi policies brought many changes for the young, women, the unemployed and Jews.

Nazi policies towards the young and women

The Nazis had their own views about the role of the young and women.

Young people

Education was targeted:
- Teachers had to swear an oath of loyalty to Hitler and join the Nazi Teachers' League. Teachers had to promote Nazi ideals in the classroom.
- The curriculum was changed to prepare students for their future roles. Hitler wanted healthy, fit men and women so fifteen per cent of time was devoted to physical education. With the boys the educational emphasis was on preparation for the military. Girls took needlework and home crafts, especially cookery, to become good homemakers and mothers.
- New subjects such as race studies were introduced to put across Nazi ideas on race and population control.

- Textbooks were rewritten to fit the Nazi view of history and racial purity. Hitler's *Mein Kampf* became a standard text.

The Nazis also wanted to control the young in their spare time. This was achieved through the Hitler Youth.

- All other youth organisations were banned and from 1936 membership of the Hitler Youth was compulsory. By 1939 there were 7 million members.
- Boys joined the German Young People at the age of ten. From fourteen to eighteen they became members of the Hitler Youth. They learned Nazi songs and ideas and took part in athletics, hiking and camping. As they got older they practised marching, map reading and military skills. Many enjoyed the comradeship.
- Girls joined the Young Girls at the age of ten. From fourteen to eighteen they joined the League of German Maidens. They did much the same as the boys, except they also learned domestic skills in preparation for motherhood and marriage and there was much less emphasis on military training.

Women

The Nazis believed in the traditional domestic role of women, which was to marry, have children and look after the home. This was summarised as the 'three Ks': *Kinder, Küche, Kirche* – children, kitchen, church.

The Nazis brought in the following changes:

- They reduced the number of women, especially married women, in employment. However, due to rearmament, more women were employed in industry after 1937.
- Hitler wanted to increase the birth rate and encouraged German women to marry and have as many children as possible. Married couples were given loans based on the number of children they had.
- They believed in the traditional natural appearance of women, with long hair, no make-up and long skirts. Women were discouraged from smoking and drinking.

Revision task

Using the information on page 41 and above, complete a copy of the table below. Use key words to summarise the changes brought in by the Nazis for young people and women in the years 1933–39.

	Schooling	Youth movements	
Young people			
	Appearance	Employment	Marriage
Women			

Exam practice

1 Explain the changes brought in by the Nazis to the position and role of women in Germany in the years 1933–39. *(8 marks)*

Employment and the standard of living

Employment

Hitler had promised to remove unemployment. This was achieved by 1938 through a variety of policies.

- The Labour Service Corps was set up. From 1935, it was compulsory for all men aged 18–25 to serve in the Corps for six months.
- Unemployed men were put to work building government-funded roads, motorways, houses, hospitals and schools.
- From 1935, all men aged 18–25 had to do two years military service.
- Rearmament provided thousands of jobs in arms factories and greatly boosted heavy industry.

Exam tip The Exam practice question above is an example of a question 2a or 2b from Unit 2. You need to:
- explain at least two changes
- explain clearly what it was that changed, using good details from your own knowledge
- decide which was the most important change, and why.

The standard of living

There is much debate about whether the German people were better or worse off under the Nazis in the years 1933–39.

Better off	Worse off
• There was more or less full employment. • The 'Strength Through Joy' movement organised leisure activities and provided the public with sports facilities, cheap holidays and entertainments. It also helped to plan the production of a 'people's car' (Volkswagen) that was cheap enough for many workers to afford. Many new motorways (autobahns) were built in the 1930s by the unemployed. • 'Beauty with Labour' was a department of 'Strength Through Joy' and tried to improve working conditions by organising the building of canteens and sports facilities for workers.	• The Labour Front replaced trade unions. Workers were not allowed to leave their jobs without government permission, and strikes were made illegal. Opposition was rare. By the late 1930s, pay had increased and workers accepted the long working hours and lack of rights because of higher pay. • The Volkswagen scheme was a swindle. People were encouraged to save five marks per week to buy their own car. By the time war broke out in 1939 not a single customer had taken delivery of a car. Moreover, the money was never refunded. • The Nazis used dubious methods to keep down the unemployment figures. The figures did not show 'invisible unemployment' which included Jews and married women forced to leave their jobs.

The persecution of minorities

The Nazis believed in the superiority of the Aryan race (non-Jewish Germans). They persecuted members of other races, and many minority groups such as Gypsies, homosexuals and mentally and physically disabled people. They persecuted any group that they thought challenged Nazi ideas. Gypsies were thought to be an inferior people. Five out of six Gypsies living in Germany in 1939 were killed by the Nazis.

The treatment of Jews

Although all groups who posed a threat to the Nazi regime were persecuted, it was the Jews who received the worst treatment of all.

In 1933, the Nazis organised a boycott of all Jewish businesses, doctors, dentists, and so on. Jewish shops were marked with the Star of David and the word '*Jude*' (Jew). In education, Jewish children were intimidated at school and Germans were taught that Jews were unclean and responsible for Germany's defeat in the First World War.

In 1935 the Nuremberg Laws were introduced in Germany. Under these laws:
• Jews could no longer be German citizens
• marriages between Jews and Aryans were forbidden
• Jews had to wear a yellow star on their clothing.

Kristallnacht

It is not clear how much most Germans knew about the persecution. However, in 1938 an event occurred that left nobody in any doubt.

In early November 1938, a Polish Jew, Herschel Grynszpan, shot a German diplomat in Paris. Hitler ordered an immediate attack on Jews and their property in Germany. Between 9 and 10 November, thousands of Jewish businesses were attacked and 200 synagogues burnt down. This was called *Kristallnacht*, 'The Night of Broken Glass'. Violence against Jews in Germany increased. Himmler, head of the SS, began to plan the expansion of concentration camps.

Revision tasks

1 Do you think that workers were better or worse off under the Nazis? Give reasons for your answer.

2 Make a copy of the table below and use the information on page 43 to complete it.

Minority group	Why Nazis persecuted them	How they were persecuted
Jews		
Gypsies		

Exam practice

SOURCE A

From a history of Germany published in 2007.

'Röhm wanted to incorporate the army into the SA and was also hoping for reforms to help the workers. He was disappointed with Hitler's close relations with army leaders and industrialists. In addition, Himmler, the leader of the SS, Hitler's personal bodyguard, wished to break away from the SA and the control of Röhm.'

1 What can you learn from Source A about the reasons for the Night of the Long Knives? *(4 marks)*

Exam tip The Exam practice question above is an example of a question 1a from Unit 2. You need to find at least one thing that the source tells you (these are called inferences). Back up each one with selected words from the source.

Key content

You need to have a good working knowledge of the following areas.
Tick off each item once you are confident in your knowledge.

- ☐ the origins of the Weimar Republic, especially the revolution of November 1918
- ☐ the early problems of the Weimar Republic, including the weaknesses of the new constitution, the Treaty of Versailles and attacks from the left and right
- ☐ the French occupation of the Ruhr and hyperinflation
- ☐ the recovery of the Republic under Stresemann in the years 1924–29
- ☐ the impact of the Great Depression on Germany, 1929–33
- ☐ Hitler's early career and the setting up of the Nazi Party
- ☐ the early development of the Nazi Party, 1920–23
- ☐ the causes, events and results of the Munich Putsch of 1923
- ☐ the changes in the Nazi Party 1924–29 and the growth in support after 1929
- ☐ the events of 1932–33 which brought Hitler to power
- ☐ the removal of opposition 1933–34, including the Reichstag fire, the Enabling Act and the Night of the Long Knives
- ☐ control of the Churches and the German people through the police state and propaganda
- ☐ changes in the position of women, the young and the unemployed
- ☐ Nazi policies towards the Jews in the years 1933–39.

Check your knowledge online with our Quick quizzes at www.hodderplus.co.uk/modernworldhistory.

In 1914, Russia was ruled by Tsar Nicholas II and went to war against Germany and Austria. The war was a disaster, with defeat after defeat and economic, political and military chaos. In 1917, there were two revolutions. These were followed by three years of civil war. The Communists emerged triumphant under Lenin, who introduced a series of reforms designed to modernise the country. Stalin won the leadership contest that followed Lenin's death and introduced a series of reforms in agriculture and industry in an attempt to modernise the Soviet economy.

Key topics

These are the key topics you need to revise. As with all examination topics you first need to learn the content so you know it well enough to answer a range of questions on this topic.

- the collapse of the Tsarist regime, 1917
- Bolshevik takeover and consolidation, 1917–24
- the nature of Stalin's dictatorship, 1924–39
- economic and social changes, 1928–39.

5.1 The collapse of the Tsarist regime, 1917

In March 1917 Tsar Nicholas II abdicated due to the growth of opposition and the impact of the First World War.

The nature of Tsarist rule

There was much opposition to Tsarist rule in the years before 1917.

The Tsarist system of government

The Russian monarch was known as the Tsar. He ruled as an **autocrat**. He believed that God had made him Tsar and that he therefore had absolute authority to rule Russia. The Tsar ruled with the support of the aristocracy (landowners), the Church, the army and the civil service.

Discontent

Various groups had become discontented before and during the First World War:
- The peasants, who formed 80 per cent of the population, often lived in extreme poverty and wanted to own their land.
- Industrial workers in large cities such as Petrograd and Moscow lived in overcrowded conditions and worked long hours for very little pay.
- **Subject nationalities** such as Poles, Lithuanians and Finns were being forced to speak the Russian language and accept Russian customs. They wanted their independence.

Key terms

Autocrat: a ruler who holds absolute power in a country and does not have to explain his actions to anyone else.
Subject nationalities: non-Russian people living in Russia.

The growth of opposition

There were several groups opposing the Tsar.

- The Social Revolutionaries were the largest and most violent group and were supported by the peasants. They wanted to carve up the huge estates of the very rich and hand them over to the peasants.
- The Bolsheviks were a small group of dedicated revolutionaries led by Lenin who wanted to overthrow the Tsar and set up a Communist government.
- The Mensheviks wanted to create a mass Communist party which would eventually overthrow the Tsar.
- The Constitutional Democrats or Cadets wanted to keep the Tsar but make him share power with a parliament or **Duma**.

> **Key term**
>
> **Duma:** a representative assembly that the Tsar consulted, but which had little power.

The impact of the First World War

In 1914 Russia went to war on the side of Britain and France and against Germany and Austria–Hungary. The war had disastrous effects for the Tsar.

> **Revision task**
>
> Make a copy of the table below and use the information on pages 45–46 to complete it.
>
> | Opposition to the Tsar | Aims |
> | --- | --- |
> | | |

Political chaos

While dealing with the war, the Tsar left the Government of Russia in the hands of his wife Alexandra. This created problems:

- Alexandra was unpopular because of her German background.
- Until his assassination in December 1916, she was under the influence of a monk called Rasputin.
- Alexandra dismissed capable ministers and refused to accept the advice of the Duma.
- She misled the Tsar about the extent of opposition in Petrograd.

Military defeat

Continued military defeat increased the unpopularity of the Tsar. The Russian soldiers were often poorly equipped due to shortages of weapons and ammunition. They suffered a series of crushing defeats at the hands of the Germans, including the Battle of Tannenburg in August 1914. They were further weakened by the long-term effects of the Brusilov offensive of 1916, which resulted in one million casualties and further hardship at home.

The Tsar took personal command of the army in 1915. This was a mistake as he was then held directly to blame for any defeats.

> **Revision task**
>
> Draw a mind map showing the effects of the First World War on Russia. On your mind map draw lines to show links between each effect. Use key words along the line to explain each link.

Economic chaos

The Russian economy could not cope with the increased demands of war.

- There was even greater overcrowding in the towns and cities, as well as low wages and rising prices.
- The Russian transport system proved totally inadequate and food often failed to reach towns and cities.
- There were serious fuel shortages by the end of 1916.

Social misery

By the end of 1916 there was discontent throughout Russia.

- In the towns and cities there were high prices and food and fuel shortages.
- In the countryside there were too few peasants to work on the land due to conscription. Consequently they suffered from increasing food shortages.
- Conditions in the army were so bad (with a lack of equipment and even boots) that an increasing number of soldiers deserted.
- There was a severe winter (even by Russian standards) in 1916–17.

> **Exam practice**
>
> 1 Explain the effects of the First World War on Russia by the beginning of 1917.
> *(8 marks)*

> **Exam tip** The Exam practice question above is an example of a question 1c from Unit 2. You need to give at least two statements which explain the effects of the First World War on Russia. You need to link each effect back to the war, not just describe it.

The fall of the Tsar

The effects of the First World War led to the February Revolution. The unrest began in February 1917 with a strike at the Puetilov steelworks in Petrograd.

- Unrest and strikes spread quickly and bread queues turned into riots.
- The workers began to form councils (called Soviets) and the leaders of the Duma (including Alexander Kerensky – see below) began to oppose the Tsar openly.
- By the end of February the troops had joined the rioters and the Tsar had no choice but to abdicate (give up power) on 3 March. The Tsar's regime was replaced by a provisional government.

The Provisional Government

After the abdication of the Tsar in 1917, the Duma appointed a Provisional Government headed at first by Prince Lvov. He was replaced by Alexander Kerensky in July of that year. Kerensky had already served in the Provisional Government as Justice Minister and War Minister. He was also Deputy Chairman of the Petrograd Soviet (worker's council). Many people already believed that the soviets were more effective as a means of government than the Duma.

Lenin and Bolsheviks

At the time of the February Revolution, Lenin, the leader of the Bolsheviks, was in exile in Germany. On his return, a month after the abdication of the Tsar, his aim was to overthrow the Provisional Government with a second revolution of the working classes.

Lenin published his views in April 1917 in the 'April Theses'. In simple terms, he said that the Bolsheviks offered 'peace, land and bread, all the power to the soviets'.

The Kornilov revolt

Alexander Kerensky began to take a grip on his opponents and Lenin was forced to leave Russia again. However, Kerensky was then challenged by the new commander of the army, General Kornilov, who wanted to impose a strict regime and crush opponents, rather like the Tsar had done.

Kerensky asked the Bolsheviks to help him defeat Kornilov, which they did. Kerensky was now in real trouble. He had lost the support of the army and was dependent upon the Petrograd Soviet (with its strong Bolshevik influence) to run Russia.

Mistakes made by the Provisional Government

The Provisional Government made several mistakes which weakened its position.

- It continued the war effort out of loyalty to Russia's allies and in return for supplies. The offensive of June 1917 was a disastrous failure and was followed by further German advances and more desertions for the Russian armed forces.
- Failure to end the war worsened the food shortages in the towns and cities.
- Because of its temporary nature, the Provisional Government would not carry out important reforms. For example, it failed to give land to the peasants, which increased discontent in the countryside.
- The Provisional Government allowed opposition parties, including Lenin and the Bolsheviks, to campaign in Russia. Real authority and support lay with the Petrograd Soviet.

Comment

This is often called the March Revolution because in 1917 Russia was using a different calendar from the West. As a result, the first Russian revolution took place in February by the Russian calendar, but March for the rest of Europe. This book will use the 'Russian' dates.

Revision task

In what ways did the following weaken the Provisional Government?
- Petrograd Soviet
- Lenin
- Kornilov revolt

Exam practice

1 Describe the key features of the Provisional Government.
(6 marks)

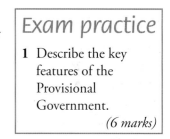

Exam tip The Exam practice question above is an example of a question 1b from Unit 2. You need to give at least two well detailed statements about the successes and failures of the Provisional Government.

5.2 Bolshevik takeover and consolidation, 1917–24

The second revolution of 1917 led to a Bolshevik takeover and three years of civil war.

The October Revolution

In October 1917 the Provisional Government was overthrown.

The Bolshevik takeover

Bolshevik support increased throughout 1917.

- In September the Bolsheviks became the largest party in the Petrograd Soviet. They also controlled the Military Committee of the Soviet, with Leon Trotsky becoming chairman.
- Trotsky used the Military Committee to plan the revolution.
- On 16 October Lenin returned to Russia (he had been forced into hiding abroad in July) and was now convinced that the time was right to overthrow the Provisional Government.
- On 24 and 25 October the Bolsheviks seized power. They took control of the key locations of Petrograd and Moscow, including the Post Office, bridges, State Bank and railway stations.
- Red Guards stormed the Winter Palace and arrested the ministers of the Provisional Government. Kerensky managed to escape and tried to rally loyal troops. When this failed, he fled into exile.

Reasons for Bolshevik success

Bolshevik success was due to various reasons.

- The Provisional Government was very unpopular. Few rallied to support Kerensky and there were no massive demonstrations demanding his return.
- Lenin played an important role. He had spent many years organising a disciplined party dedicated to revolution. His campaigning of 1917, especially his slogan 'Peace, Land and Bread', brought more support. By October, the Bolshevik Party had 800,000 members with supporters in strategic places. At least half the army supported it, as did the sailors at the important naval base at Kronstadt, near Petrograd. The major industrial centres, and the Petrograd and Moscow soviets, were also pro-Bolshevik.
- The October Revolution is often described as a classic work of planning by Trotsky. He organised the seizure of key buildings and positions in the two major cities.

> **Exam tip** Many students confuse the two revolutions of 1917. Remember the first was spontaneous opposition which led to the abdication of the Tsar. The second was a planned takeover by a group of revolutionaries.

> ## Revision tasks
>
> 1 Make a copy of the table below. Use the information on pages 48–50 to explain each reason for the success of the Bolshevik revolution in the middle column. In the last column, rate the importance of each factor on a scale of 1 to 5, with 5 as the most important. Provide an explanation of your rating.
>
> | Reason | Explanation | Rating |
> |---|---|---|
> | Unpopularity of Provisional Government | | |
> | Kornilov revolt | | |
> | Work of Lenin | | |
> | Organisation of Trotsky | | |
>
> 2 Draw a timeline to show the key events of 1917.

Imposing Bolshevik control, 1918–21

It took the Bolsheviks three years to establish control of Russia.

The Constituent Assembly

Lenin was not interested in democracy. The elections that were held late in 1917 showed that the Bolsheviks did not have the support of most Russians.

- The Constituent Assembly, which met in January 1918, contained twice as many Socialist Revolutionaries (SRs) as Bolsheviks, and the SRs opposed Lenin.
- Bolshevik Red Guards closed down the Assembly. By July 1918, the Russian Congress of Soviets had agreed a new system of government for Russia.

The result was that Lenin effectively became a dictator, and his secret police (the Cheka) began to intimidate, imprison and murder political opponents.

The Treaty of Brest-Litovsk

The Bolsheviks had always planned to pull out of the war with Germany. They agreed a ceasefire in December 1917. Trotsky was given the job of negotiating terms but his only real achievement was to hold up the Germans until March 1918, when the Bolsheviks were forced to sign the Treaty of Brest-Litovsk.

- Russia lost vast amounts of territory (see map below).
- Russia lost important coal and iron resources and about one-third of its population.
- Russia also had to pay 300 million gold roubles in compensation.

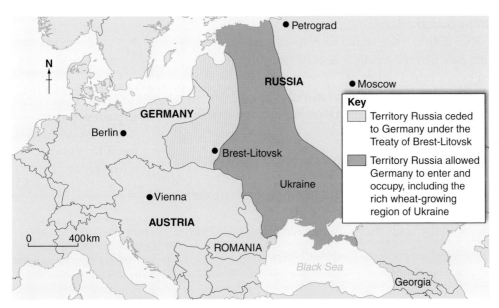

Russian losses under the Treaty of Brest-Litovsk.

The Civil War, 1918–22

The Bolsheviks had to fight a war against a number of opponents.

Who made up the opposition?

The Bolsheviks did not have the support of all Russians when they seized power. By May 1918, they had more enemies, especially after the losses of the Treaty of Brest-Litovsk. By the summer of 1918, the Bolsheviks were faced with a range of opponents united only by their opposition to the Bolsheviks. These opponents, called the Whites (in contrast to the Bolshevik Red Guards), were made up of former tsarists, Mensheviks, Socialist Revolutionaries and foreign powers opposed to the new regime in Russia.

The Bolsheviks in danger

In the early stages of the Civil War, the Bolsheviks faced several different threats.

- The Czech legion (which was made up of former prisoners of war) had seized sections of the vital Trans-Siberian railway.
- Admiral Kolchak had set up a White government in Siberia and was marching on Moscow.
- General Denikin was advancing with his army from southern Russia.
- Northern Russia, led by General Yudenich, was opposing the Bolsheviks.
- There were also risings against the Bolsheviks in Ukraine and Turkestan.
- Foreign powers supplied the Whites with arms and weapons and later landed troops to help the Whites. American, Japanese, French and British troops landed at Archangel, Murmansk and Vladivostok.

Bolshevik victory

Against what seemed to be overwhelming odds, the Bolsheviks won the Civil War. The crucial year was 1919. Under Trotsky's leadership, the Red Army defeated Kolchak and destroyed the Czech legion. Denikin's advance on Moscow was stopped and by 1920 he was being pushed back. By late 1920, White forces were completely defeated. The Bolsheviks had won due to their ruthless, disciplined commitment and the failings of their enemies.

The strengths of the Bolsheviks were:

- they had large, well organised armies under Trotsky, and good communications
- they made good use of propaganda to show that the Whites were in league with foreigners and wanted to bring back the Tsar
- together with the Cheka (secret police), they kept a ruthless control over the Bolshevik territories, making sure that most people obeyed Lenin's rule
- the Red Army was supplied by the brutal policy of 'War Communism' (see page 51), which ensured that troops and towns were fed and supplied
- they controlled major towns with factories and industries to support the war effort.

The failings of the Whites were:

- they had no aim upon which they all agreed – in some cases, they disliked each other almost as much as they opposed the Bolsheviks
- their forces were spread across a huge area and they could not co-ordinate their attacks – they were beaten one by one
- their harsh treatment of people in the lands they captured led many to support the Bolsheviks against them.

Revision task

Using the information on page 49 and above, complete a copy of the table below about the reasons for the Bolshevik victory in the Civil War.

Bolshevik strengths	White weaknesses

Exam practice

1 Explain why the Bolsheviks defeated the Whites in the Civil War of 1918–21. *(8 marks)*

Exam tip The Exam practice question above is an example of a question 1d from Unit 2. You need to:
- fully explain at least two reasons
- show clearly how each reason contributed to the Bolshevik victory
- link, or prioritise the reasons. Which do you think was the most important and why?

Creating a new society, 1918–24

The Bolsheviks introduced two very different economic policies: War Communism and the New Economic Policy.

War Communism

To defeat his opponents in the Civil War, Lenin knew that he had to make sure that his armies were fed and equipped. To achieve this, he introduced the policy of **'War Communism'**.

- Land and industry were 'nationalised' – taken over by the state.
- In the factories there was severe discipline (for example, strikers could be shot) and key items such as food and coal were rationed.
- In the countryside, peasants were forced to hand over their surplus produce (what they did not need themselves) to the Government.
- Opposition was rooted out and destroyed by the Cheka (even the royal family was executed).

Key term

War Communism: had the *appearance* of Communism, but was being carried out due to Bolshevik necessities during the Civil War.

The cost of the Civil War and War Communism

By 1921 Lenin was facing a shattered and demoralised country.

- War Communism had made the industrial workers poor and restless.
- War Communism and war damage had led to famine in the countryside – millions died in 1921.

The Kronstadt mutiny of 1921 was a turning point. The Kronstadt sailors had been leading supporters of the revolution, but they revolted against War Communism in February 1921.

Although the Kronstadt revolt was put down by Trotsky and the Civil War was being won, it was clear in 1921 that Lenin had to do something to improve people's living conditions. His solution was to replace War Communism with the New Economic Policy (NEP).

The New Economic Policy

Lenin introduced the NEP at the Bolshevik Party Congress in March 1921. Its measures were simple but controversial.

- Peasants could keep part of their surpluses to sell at a profit.
- Small factories were given back to private ownership.
- Small private businesses could be set up to trade at a profit.

Some Communists saw the NEP as a betrayal, but Lenin saw it as a temporary measure to keep the Russian people happy and get the economy moving. All of the major industries remained in state hands, and political control (under the Cheka) remained very strict.

Exam tip Do not confuse the two economic policies War Communism and NEP. Remember that the NEP was a temporary move back to capitalism.

Revision tasks

1 Make a copy of the table below. Use key words to show the difference between War Communism and the NEP.

	Aims	Key features	Effects
War Communism			
NEP			

2 Place the following events in chronological order:
- Introduction of NEP
- Kronstadt mutiny
- Treaty of Brest-Litovsk
- The end of War Communism
- Constituent Assembly

5.3 The nature of Stalin's dictatorship, 1924–39

Stalin eventually succeeded Lenin as leader of the USSR and ruthlessly removed his rivals to establish a dictatorship.

The struggle for power, 1924–28

There was a leadership contest following the death of Lenin.

The candidates

There were two main rivals:

- **Trotsky**. When Lenin died, Trotsky was the most obvious candidate to take over the leadership of the Communists. He was brilliant, talented and had an outstanding 'track record' as leader of the Bolshevik Army.
- **Stalin**. Stalin expressed no strong views – he was a hard working administrator and few expected him to win the leadership contest.

Reasons for Stalin's success

The leadership contest was eventually won by Stalin, although it took him five years to become completely established as Lenin's successor. Stalin was able to defeat his rivals for a number of reasons.

- He had taken on many important jobs (editor of the party newspaper *Pravda*, Commissar for Nationalities, Secretary-General of the party). This gave him an important power base – he had many supporters in the ranks of the party (who owed their positions to him).
- Stalin took advantage of the **Lenin Enrolment** to increase his support within the party. He also appeared as the chief mourner at Lenin's funeral while tricking Trotsky into missing it.
- Trotsky made himself unpopular. His ideas for spreading world revolution alarmed moderate Communists. He was also arrogant and offended many party members.

> **Key term**
>
> **Lenin Enrolment:** a process started in 1923, lasting until 1925, to try to get more industrial workers in the Communist Party.

> **Revision task**
>
> Draw a mind map showing the reasons why Stalin was successful in the leadership contest. Put the reasons on order, clockwise, beginning with the most important at twelve o'clock.

The purges of the 1930s

Stalin used the purges to remove all possible opposition.

Reasons

In 1934, Stalin's ally Sergei Kirov was murdered. Stalin saw this as evidence of a conspiracy and began a series of political purges (involving imprisonment and execution). Historians are now fairly sure that Stalin planned Kirov's murder to give him an excuse to purge the USSR of opponents, whom Stalin saw as traitors to himself and the USSR.

Key features

From 1934 to 1938, thousands were arrested, imprisoned, murdered or simply disappeared. They came from all areas of Soviet life.

- The Communist Party: the number of party members fell from 3.5 million in 1934 to 2 million in 1935.
- Leading party members such as Zinoviev, Kamenev and Bukharin were tortured and their families threatened. Then, at show trials, they 'confessed' and were executed.
- Many less important opponents (and even supporters who were not enthusiastic enough) were arrested and either executed or sent to labour camps (*gulags*).
- In 1937, around 25,000 army officers (including the Commander of the Red Army, Marshal Tukhachevsky) were purged.

Show trials

These began in 1936 when Stalin began purging the Communist Party of anyone who might oppose him, especially the 'Old Bolsheviks' such as Kamenev and Zinoviev. The accused were put on trial in full view of the world and forced to confess to a whole range of unlikely crimes. The confessions were important because they appeared to show that Stalin was right to carry out the purges.

Effects

The effects of the purges were mixed. Stalin was certainly secure. His new secret police (the NKVD) ruled the population with terror. Over 8 million people had been killed or sent to labour camps. However, Stalin had weakened the USSR. Many of those purged had been skilled or educated (for example, managers or army officers) and so industrial progress slowed down. The army was seriously weakened and suffered badly against the Germans in 1941.

Propaganda and censorship

Propaganda was also used to build up hero-worship of their leader. This was known as the cult of Stalin.

- The Soviet people were flooded with portraits, photographs and statues of Stalin. Every town had a Stalin Square, a Stalin Avenue or a Stalin statue in the centre.
- Poets and playwrights praised Stalin, whilst regular processions were organised through the streets of Russian towns and cities praising Stalin's achievements.
- History was re-written to show Stalin as a close friend of Lenin and a key figure in the Bolshevik revolution.

Education

In 1932 a rigid programme of education was introduced in which children were taught that Stalin was the 'Great Leader' as well as Stalin's version of history. The teaching of Communist ideology became compulsory in schools, whilst education focused on technical and scientific skills which were needed by workers involved in the Five-Year Plans (see page 55).

The constitution

Stalin made himself more secure still in 1936 with the USSR's new constitution. At first sight, it appeared more democratic – all citizens voted for members of the **Supreme Soviet**. However, it had no real power and decisions were still made by Stalin and his closest supporters.

Revision task

Make a copy of the table below and use the information in this section to complete it.

	Causes	Key features	Effects
Purges			
Propaganda			
The cult of Stalin			

Exam tip The Exam practice question on the right is an example of a question 2a or 2b from Unit 2. You need to:
- explain at least two changes
- explain clearly what it was that changed, using good details from your own knowledge
- decide which was the most important change, and why.

Exam practice

1 Were the purges the main reason for Stalin's dictatorship? You may use the following in your answer:
- the show trials
- mass arrests of Party members.

You must also include information of your own. *(16 marks)*

Exam tip The Exam practice question above is an example of a question 3a or 3b from Unit 2. You need to:
- describe in detail the way the purges helped Stalin become dictator of the USSR, using the two bullet-point items you have been given
- add at least one other cause of Stalin's dictatorship
- make links between the reasons, or prioritise which you think was the most important and why.

Key term

Supreme Soviet: an elected body of representatives (the equivalent of the British Parliament), but which had no real power. It only met for two weeks a year. It was the Communist Party under Stalin that made the important decisions.

Exam practice

2 Explain how the purges changed the USSR in the 1930s.
(8 marks)

5.4 Economic and social changes, 1928–39

Stalin believed that the USSR was under threat from non-Communist states. He also believed that the only way to make the country secure was for it to become a modern, industrial nation. His aim was to force the USSR to make fifty years' progress in ten years. There were two key aspects of Stalin's plans:

- the need to improve food production (collectivisation)
- the need to expand heavy industry (Five-Year Plans).

Collectivisation

Stalin brought in major changes to the countryside in the USSR.

Reasons

Stalin had made clear his ambitions to transform the USSR. The Five-Year Plans could work only if Soviet agriculture could raise its production massively. There were two main reasons for doing this.

- To feed the growing population of industrial workers.
- To export any surpluses to raise cash for investment in industry.

Key features

Most farms were smallholdings tended by peasant families. These holdings could never be efficient enough for Stalin's plans so he introduced the policy of collectivisation.

- Peasants effectively had to give up their land and join other families on very large farms.
- These new farms were supplied by the state with seed, tools, tractors and other machinery.
- Most of the produce went to the Government.

The real opponents of collectivisation were the kulaks. Kulaks were peasants who had become prosperous under the NEP, and they made up a large and important part of the population of the countryside. Most refused to co-operate with the new policy because they did not want to give up their land.

Effects

The effects of collectivisation were very mixed, but this policy certainly had less of a claim to success than the Five-Year Plans (see page 55). This is what happened.

- By 1941, almost all land in the USSR was collectivised.
- A huge propaganda campaign was launched to convince peasants to modernise.
- Kulaks were murdered or put in labour camps – many killed their own animals or burned their crops rather than let the Government have them.
- Much of the countryside was devastated by struggles between Stalin's agents and the kulaks.
- Although collectivisation was achieved, food production fell dramatically. In the Ukraine, there was famine in the early 1930s and at the same time food was being exported.

The long-term result of this struggle was that the peasants were battered into submission and never again seriously threatened the Communist regime.

Industrialisation

In 1928 Stalin introduced the first of his Five-Year Plans.

The Five-Year Plans

Stalin seemed to have several clear reasons for industrialising the USSR. These were:

- security
- to create a showpiece of success for the outside world
- to carry out his idea of 'socialism in one country'.

In order to achieve his aims, he came up with two Five-Year Plans for the development of the USSR. They presented incredibly ambitious targets for industrial production that had to be achieved in five years.

Although few targets were met (see right), the industries that failed to meet their targets still made huge advances.

Effects

Historians disagree about the aims and effects of the Five-Year Plans. One thing on which all historians agree is that the USSR was transformed.

- The main aim was achieved – by 1940, the USSR was in the 'first division' of industrial powers, along with Britain, Germany and the USA.
- Vast projects such as the Belomor Canal, the Dreiper Dam and the metalworks at Magnitogorsk were completed with amazing speed.
- Huge towns and factories were built from nothing, deep inside the USSR to protect them from invasion.
- Foreign technicians were brought in and enormous investment was put into education and training to produce skilled workers.
- Great pressure was put on workers to meet targets and to be 'Stakhanovites'. Stakhanov was a miner who managed to produce over 100 tonnes of coal in one shift, and was held up as a model to inspire all workers.
- The cost was high. Safety standards came second to meeting targets, discipline was harsh and many workers ended up in labour camps. All investment went into heavy industries – there were few consumer goods (clothes, luxuries).
- However, by the mid-1930s there were definite signs of improved living standards (for example, education, welfare, housing).

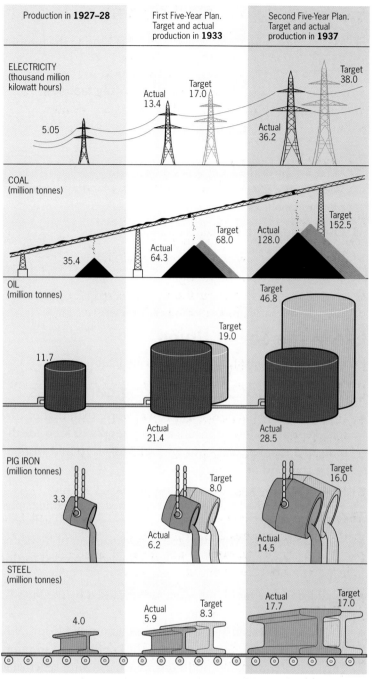

Target and actual production under the first two Five-Year Plans.

> **Exam tip** If you are asked a question about industrialisation do not write about collectivisation except if you think it affected the Five-Year Plans.

Revision tasks

1 Make a copy of the table below. Complete it using the information on pages 54–55.

	Reasons	Key features	Effects
Industrialisation			
Collectivisation			

2 Make a copy of the set of scales shown here. Write the successes and failures of Stalin's economic policies on the pans.

3 Overall, do you think Stalin's economic policies were a success? Explain your answer.

Successes of economic policies

Failures of economic policies

Exam practice

1 Explain how industry changed under Stalin in the years 1928–39.
(8 marks)

Exam tip This is a question 2a or 2b from Unit 2. You will need to:
- fully explain at least two changes
- make links between each change
- link, or prioritise the changes. Which do you think was the most important and why?

Life in the Soviet Union

Everyday life was transformed in the years 1928–39.

Living conditions and working conditions

- For the mass of the peasantry life was worse than that of town workers. The state kept prices low to ensure a cheap supply of food for the towns. As a result, more and more peasants moved to the towns to find work and, hopefully, a better standard of living.
- Some workers were promoted into management jobs in industry. For example, over one and a half million workers gained management posts under the first Five-Year Plan.
- Some workers also benefited from the expansion of higher education which enabled them to gain the technical knowledge needed for higher management posts.
- In addition, the rapid industrialisation caused by the Five-Year Plans removed any areas of unemployment.
- The downside was that the urban population rose from 29 million in 1929 to 40 million only four years later. This, in turn, led to poor living conditions. Furthermore, working conditions were harsh with strict rules about discipline and punctuality.
- As peasants flooded into towns and cities, all the basic amenities became overcrowded. Trams and buses were jam packed. Flats had to be shared by several families. Often, there was one family per room and they had to share the bathroom and kitchen. In Moscow, only 6 per cent of families lived in more than one room.

Women

- Women made progress in the area of employment. They were encouraged to work in almost all areas. Some women took on jobs like engineering, which had once been done only by men. However, life remained hard for most Soviet women. They were expected to work full time, as well as bring up a family. Help was provided by state nurseries and crèches.
- Politically, women still remained second-class citizens, with less than 20 percent of the Communist Party membership being women and very few women rising to high positions in the party or government.

Ethnic minorities

Although Stalin was from the Georgians, an ethnic minority group within the Soviet Union, he had no sympathy for the plight of these non-Russian groups and gave them a hard time. He wanted to turn them into 'Soviet citizens' rather than, for example, Ukrainians or Georgians.

- Minority groups were discouraged from speaking their own languages and practising their own customs and traditions.
- They were often discriminated against with few gaining high positions in industry or the armed forces.
- They were targets of Stalin's purges. From 1935 the Soviet Government carried out 'cleansing' operations in border regions. Finnish, Latvian and Estonian families were deported from the Leningrad region to Kazakhstan and Siberia.

Exam practice

SOURCE A
From a history of Russia and the USSR published in 2006.
'Lenin and Trotsky played crucial roles in the Bolshevik takeover. Trotsky was the organiser, carefully planning the revolution. Lenin showed tremendous vitality and enthusiasm and gave the Bolsheviks simple slogans which were easily understood by the Russian people. He was able to exploit the mistakes of the Provisional Government.'

1 What can you learn from Source A about the reasons for the success of the Bolshevik takeover in October 1917? *(4 marks)*

Revision task
Draw a mind map on one side of A3 paper to show the changes that Stalin brought to the USSR in the years 1928–39. Include the purges, propaganda, the cult of Stalin, industrialisation, collectivisation, living and working conditions and the role of women.

Exam tip The Exam practice question above is an example of a question 1a from Unit 2. You need to find at least one thing that the source tells you (these are called inferences). Back up each one with selected words from the source.

Key content

You need to have a good working knowledge of the following areas.
Tick off each item once you are confident in your knowledge.

- ❑ the nature of Tsarist rule and the growth of opposition groups
- ❑ the impact of the First World War on Russia, especially military defeat and economic and social effects
- ❑ the key features of the February Revolution of 1917
- ❑ the mistakes and weaknesses of the Provisional Government
- ❑ the reasons for the success of the Bolshevik takeover
- ❑ the key features of Lenin's government, especially the Treaty of Brest-Litovsk and the Constituent Assembly
- ❑ the reasons for Bolshevik success in the Civil War
- ❑ the key features of War Communism and the NEP
- ❑ how and why Stalin succeeded Lenin as leader
- ❑ how Stalin established his dictatorship, especially the purges and propaganda
- ❑ the reasons for, key features of and effects of collectivisation and industrialisation
- ❑ the changes in living and working conditions and the role of women.

Check your knowledge online with our Quick quizzes at www.hodderplus.co.uk/modernworldhistory.

6.2 US society, 1919–29

Like its economy, American society was full of contrasts in the 1920s. There were very real advances for some Americans – they owned cars and electrical goods, and enjoyed themselves as never before.

The 'Roaring Twenties'

This was the name given to life in the USA in the 1920s.

Consumerism

The economic boom of the 1920s was partly encouraged by the growth of consumerism. This meant the growing demand for everyday, often household, goods by many Americans. Increased demand for consumer goods was due to several factors:

- By 1927 two-thirds of US homes had electricity. This stimulated the demand for electrical goods such as washing machines and vacuum cleaners. The growth in female employment (see below) also increased the need for these labour-saving devices.
- Hire purchase schemes made it easier to buy goods on credit.
- The popularity of entertainment meant more and more Americans bought radios.
- For the majority of workers in industry, wages increased. Between 1923 and 1929 the average wage rose by eight per cent. In other words, workers had more spare money to spend on consumer goods.

Entertainment

During the 1920s, films became a national obsession. Millions of Americans went to the cinema each week to watch new stars such as Buster Keaton and Charlie Chaplin. Hollywood became the centre of a multi-million dollar industry.

The 'Jazz Age'

The 1920s is known as the 'Jazz Age' because the popular music of the time was jazz. The writer F. Scott Fitzgerald coined the phrase in 1922 in his book *The Beautiful and Damned*.

Jazz was not new. It originated with African American slaves who were encouraged to sing in order to increase production. They used washboards, cans, pickaxes and percussion to produce their own distinctive brand of music. Their music was given various names including 'blues', 'rag' or 'boogie-woogie'. By changing the beat and creating particular rhythms, it was changed into jazz.

Women

After the First World War, women were given the vote in the USA. At this time, they gained greater freedom by working and earning their own money. One symbol of this new independence was the flappers – independent young women named after their short skirts. They cut their hair short, wore make-up and smoke and drank in public. They also openly danced with men in public (especially the new craze, the Charleston), listened to jazz and drove cars and motorbikes.

However, although about 8 million women were now working, mainly as teachers or secretaries, more women were housewives doing the work they had always done.

Revision task

In fewer than five words, define:
- the 'Roaring Twenties'
- the 'Jazz Age'
- a flapper.

Exam practice

1 Describe the key features of the 'Roaring Twenties'.
    (6 marks)

Exam tip The Exam practice question above is an example of a question 1b from Unit 2. You need to give at least two well detailed statements about the Roaring Twenties.

Prohibition and gangsters

One of the most controversial features of the USA in the 1920s was prohibition.

Prohibition

By the end of the First World War, there was a strong temperance (anti-alcohol) movement in the USA. Temperance groups pressured the Government to pass the Eighteenth Amendment to the US Constitution – prohibition. Brewing or selling alcohol was now illegal in the USA.

Prohibition was a failure. It didn't stop the alcohol trade – it simply drove it underground. **Bootleggers** made a lot of money smuggling alcohol into the USA, or through illegal brewing. Secret bars, called speakeasies, were easy to find. Even the American President was known to drink.

Gangsters

Gangs of criminals began to run bootlegging and other forms of crime (gambling, drugs, prostitution) almost like a business. These gangs would sometimes fight with each other for control of the trade.

The most notorious gang leader was Al Capone, who virtually controlled the city of Chicago by bribing the mayor and other politicians. Capone was almost certainly responsible for the St Valentine's Day Massacre in 1929 when six members of a rival gang were killed.

Racism and intolerance

At the same time as some young Americans were experiencing liberation, others were facing intolerance and racism.

The Red Scare

The Communist revolution in Russia (see Chapter 5) alarmed some Americans, particularly leading industrialists. They saw the USA's trade unions as a threat which could lead to revolution.

The **radicals** in the USA's immigrant communities were immediate targets. They were suspected of planning revolution. Police, soldiers and ex-servicemen disrupted meetings and raided offices, and thousands of people were arrested. The Government was involved in, and supported, this campaign.

It was nothing like the scale of what was to come in Nazi Germany, but this was an unpleasant aspect of the USA in the 1920s. In one extreme case, two Italian radicals, Sacco and Vanzetti, were executed for murder. Most historians are now convinced that they were innocent of this crime (see below).

The Sacco and Vanzetti case

Sacco and Vanzetti were Italian immigrants. They were known anarchists who hated the American system of government. In 1920, they were charged with the murder of two guards during an armed robbery.

- Sixty-one eyewitnesses identified them as the killers.
- The defence found 107 witnesses who swore to seeing the men elsewhere. These were mostly Italian immigrants.
- The two men were found guilty and executed in 1927.
- In 1977, the verdict against the men was declared unjust because the judge presiding over the case had been prejudiced against the men's political views.

> ## Exam practice
>
> 1 Explain how prohibition changed US society in the 1920s. *(8 marks)*

> **Exam tip** The Exam practice question above is an example of a question 2a or 2b from Unit 2. You need to:
> - explain at least two changes
> - explain clearly what it was that changed, using good details from your own knowledge
> - make links between these changes, or decide which was the most important change, and why.

> ## Key terms
>
> **Bootleggers:** people who carried liquor into the USA from Canada or Mexico. The name comes from the fact that they sometimes hid the bottles inside their knee-length boots.
> **Radicals:** people or groups (sometimes within other groups) who hold extreme political views.

The Monkey Trial

Most people living in the towns and cities of the USA accepted Charles Darwin's theory of evolution, which suggested that over a period of millions of years human beings had evolved from ape-like creatures. However, these views were not accepted by many people in rural areas, especially in the so-called '**Bible Belt**' states such as Tennessee. Many in these areas were known as fundamentalists. They held strong Protestant Christian beliefs, including the belief that the Biblical account of God creating humans on the sixth day was literally true.

Six US states chose to ban the teaching of Darwin's theory of evolution in their schools. A biology teacher called John Scopes decided to challenge this ban. He deliberately taught evolution in his class in Tennessee in order to be arrested and put on trial. Scopes was convicted of breaking the law. However, the trial was a disaster for the public image of the fundamentalists. Their leader, William Jennings Bryan, was shown to be confused and ignorant whilst the media mocked the beliefs of those who opposed the theory of evolution.

Racism

Forty-one of the white-controlled state governments, fearing the power of African Americans, introduced laws to control the freedom of African American people in the years after 1865. These were known as the **Jim Crow** laws. The state government **segregated** African American people from white people in schools, parks, hospitals, swimming pools, libraries and other public places. After the First World War new Jim Crow laws were passed in some states so that there were segregated taxis, race tracks and boxing matches.

The Ku Klux Klan

The Klan was another example of the darker side of the 1920s in the USA. It was originally formed to terrorise African American slaves after they had been given freedom in the nineteenth century. As well as African Americans, the Klan also attacked Catholics and Jews. It was a movement of mainly poor whites concerned about their livelihoods in 1920s USA.

Key terms

Bible Belt: those states in America where Protestant fundamentalism is strong.

Jim Crow: a name made popular by a white American comedian who made fun of African Americans. Originally, Jim Crow was a character in an old song. This name became linked to the southern laws ensuring that African American people remained inferior.

Segregation: keeping a group separate from the rest of society, usually on the basis of race or religion. Segregation was seen in separate schools, transport and housing.

Revision task

Using the information on page 61 and above, complete a copy of the table below.

a) In column 2, use key words to summarise each example of racism and intolerance in the USA in the 1920s.

b) In column 3, give each example a rating out of 5 to show how serious it was, with 5 being the most serious.

	Key features	How serious (1–5)
The Ku Klux Klan		
Sacco and Vanzetti		
The Monkey Trial		
The Red Scare		

6.3 The USA in depression, 1929–33

The boom of the 1920s came to a sudden end with the Wall Street Crash of 1929 which was followed by the Great Depression.

Causes and consequences of the Wall Street Crash

The Wall Street Crash was a result of long-term weaknesses in the US economy and the short-term problems of the stock market.

Weaknesses in the US economy

There were worrying weaknesses in the American economy during the period building up to the Crash.

- Some major industries did not grow in the 1920s (for example, coal and textiles).
- Farmers had produced too much food and prices were very low.
- Many ordinary Americans did not share in the boom. African Americans, in particular, suffered from discrimination, getting the worst jobs.
- Some industries were struggling against foreign competition.
- Other industries could not export goods because of tariffs in other countries. Often these tariffs were simply a reaction to American tariffs already in place.

Short-term causes of the Crash

Short-term causes related to shares. Many ordinary Americans bought shares in companies. Normally this is good for business. However, in the USA in the 1920s the rush to buy shares caused problems.

- Many people bought and sold shares to make quick profits instead of keeping their money invested in the same businesses for some time. They were speculators, not investors.
- Companies were forced by shareholders to pay out profits to shareholders rather than reinvesting the profits.
- Americans borrowed money on credit to buy their shares.

These kind of share dealings depended on confidence that share prices would continue to rise. Once people started worrying about the long-term weaknesses in the American economy, disaster struck. In September 1929, the prices of shares began to edge down – slowly to start with – but people soon began to realise that the shares they owned were worth less than the loans they had used to buy them in the first place. All of a sudden, everyone tried to get rid of their shares, selling them for less and less. The worst day was 'Black Tuesday', 29 October 1929. As a result, share prices collapsed.

The immediate effects

The effects of the Crash were disastrous.

- Many individuals were bankrupt – they could not pay back the loans they used to buy their (now worthless) shares.
- Some homeowners lost their homes as they could not pay their mortgages.
- Even some of those who had savings lost their money when banks collapsed.
- Many farmers suffered a similar fate as banks tried to get back their loans.

The confidence of individuals was shattered. Many faced unemployment, and those in work faced reduced hours and wages. They tightened their belts and stopped spending.

Exam practice

1. Was the weakness of the US economy the main reason for the Wall Street Crash? You may use the following in your answer:
   - over-production of food
   - foreign competition.

   You must also include information of your own. *(16 marks)*

Exam tip The Exam practice question above is an example of a question 3a or 3b from Unit 2. You need to:
- describe in detail how the weakness of the US economy helped to cause the Wall Street Crash using the two bullet-point items you have been given
- add at least one other cause of the Wall Street Crash from your own knowledge
- make links between the reasons, or prioritise which you think was the most important and why.

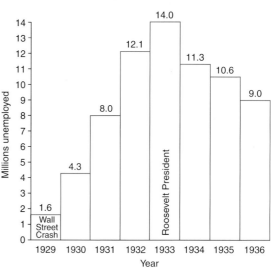

Unemployment, 1929–36.

Big institutions also suffered. About 11,000 banks stopped trading between 1929 and 1933. At the same time, demand for goods of all types fell. As a result, production fell and so did wages and jobs.

Unemployment rose dramatically, as shown in the graph on page 63.

Revision tasks

1 In your view, what were the main causes of the Wall Street Crash? Copy and complete a summary table like the one below, using the information from page 63 and above.

Short-term causes	Long-term causes

2 How did the Crash affect Americans? Think of four to six key words for your answer.

Exam practice

1 Explain the immediate effects of the Wall Street Crash.
(8 marks)

Exam tip The Exam practice question above is an example of a question 1c from Unit 2. You need to give at least two statements which explain the effects of the Wall Street Crash. You need to link each effect back to the Crash, not just describe it.

Government reaction, 1929–32

President Hoover has often been criticised for his failure to deal with the immediate effects of the Great Depression.

President Hoover's actions

Hoover eventually had to take action to deal with the effects of the Depression.
- He reduced taxes, but this mainly helped the wealthy.
- He tried to help farmers with the Federal Farming Board, which purchased surplus crops in an attempt to keep up prices. This was not enough. The farmers wanted help paying their mortgages.
- He agreed the Smoot-Hawley tariff, putting heavy duties on imports to try to protect US industries.
- The Federal Home Loan Bank Act, passed in July 1932, was designed to stimulate home building and increase home ownership. To do this, Hoover set up twelve regional banks with a fund of $125 million to help fund discounted home loans.

Was Hoover unfairly blamed?

Most Americans blamed President Hoover for the Crash.
- Hoover insisted that the situation was not too serious, and that 'prosperity is just around the corner'. This unfounded optimism upset many Americans.
- Hoover believed in '**rugged individualism**' and showed little sympathy for the poor, starving Americans living in shanty towns, which were nicknamed 'Hoovervilles'.
- He refused to provide federal aid for the unemployed or support a programme of public works to provide jobs for them.

Resentment among the people

With wages falling and unemployment rising, resentment grew among the American people. Hoover became very unpopular in 1932 when he ordered the US army to disperse the Bonus Marchers. These were veterans who had fought in the First World War. They had marched to Washington demanding early payment of a monetary bonus due to be paid to them in 1945. They wanted it paid early to offset the effects of the Depression. They even built a 'Hooverville' or shanty town on the edge of Washington DC. When the army tried to clear the Bonus Marchers, many were injured and two children were killed.

Revision task

List the reasons that you can find on this page to support Source 1 below.

SOURCE 1

Slogan of protesting farmers in Iowa.

'In Hoover we trusted, now we are busted!'

Key term

Rugged individualism: the notion that people should overcome problems and succeed by their own efforts and hard work, not by receiving help from the government.

The impact of the Depression on people's lives

The Depression affected people both in the cities and the countryside.

The Depression in the cities

By 1933 almost one-third of the American workforce was unemployed. Once a person became unemployed it became almost impossible to secure another job. As people lost jobs they lost their homes, with some having to move into 'Hoovervilles'. Many of the unemployed simply wandered the streets or slept in doorways or cardboard boxes. Others drifted across the USA as **hobos**. It was estimated that in 1932 there were more than 2 million hobos.

African Americans were particularly badly affected. When the Depression began African Americans were the first to lose their jobs. Their unemployment rate had risen to 50 per cent by 1933. In addition, those who managed to keep their jobs suffered wage cuts.

The Depression also had a tremendous effect on family life.
- Young people were reluctant to take on the commitment of marriage and the number of marriages fell, as did the birth rate.
- The suicide rate rose dramatically from 12.6 per 100,000 in 1926 to 17.4 per 100,000 by 1930.
- In some states schools were closed for ten months in the year because there was not enough money to pay the teachers.

> **Key term**
>
> **Hobos:** tramps or drifters.

The Depression in the countryside

Agriculture already faced problems in the 1920s (see page 59). However, as the Depression took hold these problems intensified.
- There were more bankruptcies as farmers were unable to sell their produce. Crops were often left to rot in the ground. Many farmers and labourers left the countryside to seek work in the towns.
- The drought of 1931 only worsened the situation. For most of the 1930s there was low rainfall and a subsequent fall in corn yields.
- The states worst hit by the drought were Texas, Oklahoma, Colorado, Kansas and New Mexico. The soil turned to dust and when the winds came there were dust storms. The affected area of 20 million hectares became known as the 'dust bowl'.
- The formation of the dust bowl forced more than 1 million people to leave their homes and seek work in the fruit-growing areas of the West coast.

> **Exam tip** Remember that the Depression affected both the cities and the countryside.

Revision tasks

1 'Hoover deserved all the criticism he got.' Make a copy of the table below and use the information in this section to complete each column.

Criticisms of Hoover	Defence of Hoover

2 Make a copy of the Venn diagram below. Complete the diagram by using key words to show the effects of the Depression on the cities and on the countryside. Write the effects on *both* areas in the overlapping section of the diagram.

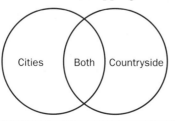

Cities   Both   Countryside

6.4 Roosevelt and the New Deal, 1933–41

The election of Roosevelt as President brought about a change of policy known as the New Deal.

The nature of the New Deal

Roosevelt introduced a series of measures to tackle the problems of unemployment.

The election of 1932

Franklin D. Roosevelt was well educated and a talented, passionate politician. He had complete faith in his ideas for bringing the USA out of the Depression. During the presidential election campaign of 1932, his key phrase was his offer of a 'New Deal' for the American people. He won the election by a large margin: Roosevelt polled nearly 23 million votes compared to fewer than 16 million votes for Hoover. His victory was due to:

- his own promises of a New Deal
- the unpopularity of Hoover's policies in the years 1929–32.

Roosevelt's 'Hundred Days'

Due to the banking crisis and high level of unemployment, Roosevelt was determined to act quickly. From 9 March to 16 June 1933 (the 'Hundred Days') he managed to get the US **Congress** to pass a huge amount of legislation. This is summarised in the table below.

> **Key term**
>
> **Congress:** the American representative assemblies (the equivalent of Parliament in Britain). There are two houses, the Senate and the House of Representatives. Roosevelt had majority Democrat support in both houses.

Hundred Days legislation, 9 March–16 June 1933		
Legislation	Problem	Action
Emergency Banking Act Securities Exchange Act	Americans had little confidence in the banks and might withdraw all their savings – this would lead to collapse of the banking system.	The Government declared a 'bank holiday' and closed all banks. It officially backed 5,000 banks and reassured the American people that their money was safe, restoring confidence in the banking system when the 'sound' banks were reopened eight days later. The Securities Exchange Act was set up to regulate the stock market to make sure that the speculation which caused the 1929 crash could not happen again.
Federal Emergency Relief Administration (FERA)	Poverty and unemployment	500 million dollars allocated to help relieve suffering of poor (food, clothing, etc.); seed and equipment for farmers; schemes to create jobs.
Civilian Conservation Corps (CCC)	Unemployment among young men	Men aged 18–25 given six months' work. Had to send most of their pay home to parents/wives. About 300,000 joined in 1933; by 1940, there were two million.
Public Works Administration (PWA) (became Works Progress Administration in 1935)	Unemployment	Paid for public works projects (for example, schools, roads, hospitals) and used unemployed workers.
Agricultural Adjustment Administration (AAA)	Rural poverty, unemployment and low crop prices	Advised farmers on marketing and farming techniques and helped solve problem of overproduction by government buying up produce. Farmers became more organised but wealthy farmers gained most.

Hundred Days legislation, 9 March–16 June 1933		
Legislation	Problem	Action
National Industrial Recovery Act (NIRA)	General economic condition of the USA	Set up National Recovery Administration (NRA), which set standards on working practices (hours, child labour). This helped create more jobs. Employers in the scheme displayed the eagle symbol of government approval and the Government encouraged people to use these firms. Over two million employers joined the scheme.
Tennessee Valley Authority (TVA)	Agricultural overproduction and regular flooding had ruined livelihoods of farm workers in the Tennessee Valley. No alternative jobs in industry. Area covered parts of six states and was too big for any one state to deal with.	Huge public works projects: dams, irrigation, canals and water transport. Hydroelectric power created thousands of jobs. Farmers given loans and training in soil conservation. New housing built.

The Second New Deal

As well as passing new legislation in his first hundred days of office, in later years Roosevelt updated some laws and created further legislation where it was needed.

- In 1935 the Works Progress Administration (WPA) replaced the Public Works Administration (PWA). It extended the range of employment provided, from building work to the Federal Theatre Project, which gave work to unemployed artists and writers.
- The National Labor Relations Act or Wagner Act (1935) forced employers to recognise trade unions after the National Recovery Administration was declared illegal by American courts. This law meant that workers kept the protection which the NRA had given them.
- The Social Security Act (1935) provided federal aid for the elderly and set up an unemployment insurance scheme. However, the provisions were still far less comprehensive than those in Germany or Britain.

Exam tip You will be expected to know the purpose and key features of these New Deal policies.

Revision tasks

1 Using a few key words, explain why Roosevelt won the Presidential election campaign of 1932.

2 Make a copy of the table below. Give the full title of the measures listed and use a few key words to explain what each did.

Measure	Full title	What it did
PWA		
NRA		
AAA		
CCC		
FERA		

Exam practice

1 Explain how Roosevelt's New Deal policies changed the plight of the unemployed in the years 1933–41.

(8 marks)

Exam tip The Exam practice question above is an example of a question 2a or 2b from Unit 2. You need to:
- explain at least two changes affecting unemployed people
- explain clearly what it was that changed
- add good details from your own knowledge.

Opposition to the New Deal

There were a number of groups in the USA who were critical of the New Deal.

Business leaders

They were unhappy about various aspects of the New Deal:
- regulations on working conditions
- the growth of trade unions and their increasing power
- the huge cost of the welfare programmes (which came from taxes paid by Americans).

The states

Some states were concerned about the New Deal because:
- measures like the TVA cut right across the rights of individual states
- they feared that the Federal Government was becoming too powerful.

Politicians

Some politicians opposed the New Deal.
- Republicans (not surprisingly) bitterly opposed the Democrat Roosevelt.
- Even some conservative Democrats opposed him.
- Some radicals in the USA, like Huey Long, believed the New Deal did not go far enough.

The Supreme Court

The Supreme Court clashed with Roosevelt.
- Its judges (mainly old and Republican) ruled that several of the New Deal measures were illegal.
- Matters came to a head in 1937 when Roosevelt wanted to appoint six new judges to alter the political balance of the Court in favour of the Democrats. This plan failed but afterwards Supreme Court opposition lessened.

> ## Revision task
> Make a copy of this pie chart (right). Prioritise the four different groups who opposed the New Deal by placing the most important in the largest section down to the least important in the smallest. Use key words in each section to explain your decisions.

The extent of recovery

The New Deal did bring some improvements but was not a total success.

Assessing the New Deal

> **Exam tip** Ensure you give a balanced judgement on the achievements of the New Deal. It was neither a total success nor a total failure.

Weaknesses	Successes
<ul><li>When Roosevelt cut back his programmes in 1937 unemployment rose dramatically.</li><li>He never fully conquered unemployment in the 1930s; unemployment was only solved by the USA's entry into the Second World War in 1941.</li><li>The USA's trade (and the world's trade) did not recover.</li><li>Roosevelt failed to convince even his own supporters of the need to change the organisation of the Supreme Court to stop it opposing his reforms.</li><li>African Americans gained relatively little from the New Deal.</li></ul>	<ul><li>In the USA the Depression did not lead to extreme movements such as Communism or fascism taking hold. Roosevelt restored the American people's faith in democracy.</li><li>Many millions of jobs were created and vital relief (food, shelter, clothing) was supplied to the poor.</li><li>Agriculture and industry benefited from efficient infrastructure (roads, services).</li></ul>

Revision tasks

1 Make a copy of this set of scales (right). On the scales, summarise the successes and weaknesses of the New Deal.

2 Overall, do you think the New Deal was successful in solving the social and economic problems of the USA 1933–41? Use a few key words to record your opinion.

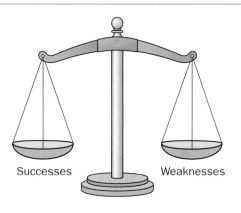

Successes   Weaknesses

Exam practice

SOURCE A

From a history of the USA published in 2009.

'The American economy greatly benefited from the First World War. In the 1920s America enjoyed an economic boom which was encouraged by the policies of the Republican presidents as well as the advanced techniques that the car industry began to use. There was a rapid growth in new industries and a dramatic rise in the values of shares on the US stock market.'

1 What can you learn from Source A about the reasons for the economic boom of the 1920s? *(4 marks)*

Exam tip The Exam practice question above is an example of a question 1a from Unit 2. You need to find at least one thing that the source tells you (these are called inferences). Back up each one with selected words from the source.

Key content

You need to have a good working knowledge of the following areas.
Tick off each item once you are confident in your knowledge.

- ❏ the causes and consequences of the economic boom
- ❏ mass production and the Ford Motor Company
- ❏ hire purchase and the stock market boom
- ❏ declining industries and the problems of agriculture
- ❏ Hollywood, jazz and changes in entertainment
- ❏ changes in the position of women, especially the flappers
- ❏ prohibition and the gangsters
- ❏ the Jim Crow laws and the Ku Klux Klan
- ❏ Sacco and Vanzetti and the Monkey Trial
- ❏ the long- and short-term causes of the Wall Street Crash
- ❏ the immediate effects of the Crash
- ❏ Hoover's attempts to deal with the Depression
- ❏ the effects of the Depression on cities and the countryside
- ❏ the key features of Roosevelt's First and Second New Deal
- ❏ opposition to the New Deal
- ❏ the successes and weaknesses of the New Deal.

Check your knowledge online with our Quick quizzes at www.hodderplus.co.uk/modernworldhistory.

During this period Britain experienced major social reforms under the Liberal governments, became involved in the First World War and experienced the only ever British general strike.

Key topics

These are the key topics you need to revise. As with all examination topics you first need to learn the content so you know it well enough to answer a range of questions on this topic.

- The Liberals, votes for women and social reform, c.1903–14
- the part played by Britain on the Western Front, c.1914–18
- the Home Front and social change, 1914–18
- economic and social change, 1918–29.

7.1 The Liberals, votes for women and social reform, c.1903–14

In the years before 1914 the Liberals brought in a series of social welfare measures whilst women campaigned for the right to vote.

Votes for women

At the beginning of the twentieth century, women in Britain played little part in political life. They were not able to vote in general elections or stand for Parliament. Three different societies campaigned for the vote for women in the years before 1914.

The National Union of Women's Suffrage Societies (NUWSS)

The National Union of Women's Suffrage Societies was set up in 1897 by Millicent Fawcett and had 500 or more branches throughout the country. Fawcett was a suffragist. Suffragists believed that women would get the vote eventually. The NUWSS issued pamphlets, presented petitions and organised marches and meetings. Fawcett thought it was crucial to keep the issue of women's suffrage in the public eye.

The Women's Freedom League (WFL)

The Women's Freedom League was set up in 1907 by Charlotte Despard. Members were not as peaceful as the suffragists and were prepared to break the law as long as it did not lead to violence. Their methods included the following:

- In 1911 members refused to take part in the census, the official population count. They broke the law by refusing to fill in the census form.
- Others chained themselves to the railings outside the House of Commons.
- Members refused to pay taxes, arguing that they were not represented in Parliament. For this, their property was sold to pay what was owing.
- Muriel Matters, a member of the WFL, hired an airship and flew over the Houses of Parliament, throwing out carrots and propaganda leaflets.

> ### Comment
>
> *On 9 February 1907 about 4,000 women walked from Hyde Park to the Exeter Hall in the Strand. Unfortunately it poured with rain all day and the long skirts and dresses of the women were soon covered with mud. This was why it was nicknamed the 'mud march'. The women who took part showed great bravery in the face of some hostile male onlookers.*

The Women's Social and Political Union (WSPU)

In 1903 Mrs Emmeline Pankhurst founded a new organisation, the Women's Social and Political Union, which was determined to use more extreme, even militant, methods to get publicity and secure the vote more quickly. The *Daily Mail* nicknamed these more extreme campaigners 'suffragettes' and the name stuck. They used a variety of methods:

- WSPU militancy began in 1905 when they interrupted meetings of Liberals and were arrested.
- On 5 July 1909, the imprisoned suffragette Marion Wallace Dunlop went on hunger strike.
- In March 1912 the WSPU began a stone-throwing campaign in the centre of London to gain even more publicity for the cause of votes for women.
- On 5 June 1913, Emily Wilding Davison, in order to get maximum publicity, decided to rush out and pin a suffragette banner on the King's horse, Anmer, while he was competing in the Derby at Epsom race course. As the horses rounded Tattenham Corner, Davison rushed in front of Anmer, only to be hit by the horse and killed.
- In the years 1912–14 the suffragettes escalated their violence. They cut telephone wires, set fire to derelict buildings and post boxes, poured purple dye into reservoirs, poured acid on the greens of golf courses and slashed paintings in art galleries. They frequently attacked and assaulted leading Liberals, especially Prime Minister Asquith.

> **Exam tip** The WSPU is generally well known. Do not forget the methods and activities of the other two societies.

How did the authorities react?

The Liberals had to deal with the problems of hunger-striking and increasing suffragette militancy.

- The prison authorities were afraid that a suffragette might die in prison. This would give the suffragette movement even more publicity, so they began force-feeding the prisoners.
- More and more suffragettes were arrested, went on hunger strike and were force-fed. In 1913 the Government introduced the Temporary Discharge Bill which was nicknamed the 'Cat and Mouse Act'. Prisoners on hunger strike were released when very ill and sent back to prison when they had recovered.

> **Comment**
>
> *In many respects the activities of the suffragettes, designed to gain the vote for women, had the opposite effect. Their extreme militant activities convinced many people that women were not responsible enough to have the vote. The suffragettes also made it difficult for Asquith, the Prime Minister, to introduce any such measure without looking as if he was giving in to violence.*

Revision task

Make a copy of the table below and use the information on page 70 and above to complete it. Give each society a rating out of 5 (with 5 being very effective) for the methods used. Briefly explain each decision.

Society	Leader	Methods	Rating (1–5)
NUWSS			
WFL			
WSPU			

Child welfare measures and OAPs

The Liberals introduced a series of measures to help the young and the old.

Child welfare measures

The Liberals believed it was very important for the children of the poor to be looked after properly. If parents could not do this, then it was the responsibility of the state. They brought in a series of reforms, including:

The Battle of the Somme, 1916

General Sir Douglas Haig, the British commander, decided to launch a major attack against the Germans along the River Somme. He hoped that by using heavy artillery he would be able to weaken the German front line and so allow the British troops to advance. He also hoped to relieve the pressure on Verdun. This is what happened.

- The battle began with a five-day bombardment of German positions along a 30 km front.
- The German troops had prepared dugouts deep underground in order to survive the bombardment.
- On 1 July, 200,000 Allied soldiers attacked the German trenches along the Somme. British troops were ordered to walk not run since each man was carrying up to 30 kg of equipment.
- In the ten minutes between the end of the bombardment and the British attack, the Germans were able to return to their trenches and machine guns.
- On the first day of the battle, the British lost 20,000 men with another 40,000 wounded.

The Battle of the Somme ended in the middle of November 1916. Only 14 km of land had been gained by the Allies, at a cost of 600,000 casualties. At the end of 1916, there was still no breakthrough on the Western Front.

The wisdom of British tactics has been debated ever since. Sir Douglas Haig, the British general in charge of the offensive, has been ridiculed by many writers, but his reputation has been defended by others.

The end of the war

The Western Front, 1918: victory for the Allies

In April 1917, the USA joined the Allies in the war against Germany. The Germans knew it would take time for the USA to recruit and train an army, so they drew up plans to win a swift victory before the full impact of the American army was felt on the Western Front.

By March 1918, the Russian army had been defeated on the Eastern Front. The Germans could now move a million of their own men to the Western Front.

- Ludendorff, the German commander, decided that since he now had many more men than the Allies, he must make an all-out attack on the Western Front before large numbers of American troops arrived in Europe.
- On 21 March 1918, the Ludendorff offensive began and the Germans advanced rapidly; they had soon moved forward 65 km along a 130 km front.

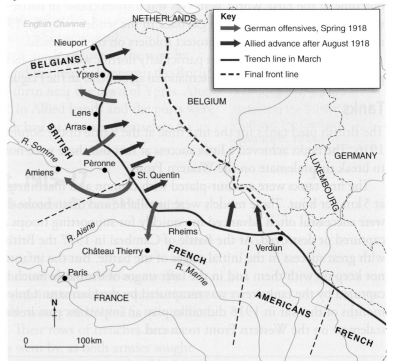

Europe in the final stages of the war.

- They reached the River Marne in July and once again the French capital looked as if it might fall to the Germans.

The Allied commander at the time, General Foch, began his counter-attack on 18 July and with the help of newly arrived American troops was able to reverse the German advance.

- In August, the British defeated the Germans at Amiens with the help of tanks.
- More victories followed in Flanders (for example, at Ypres).

On 4 October, with the German army in full retreat, Ludendorff asked the Allies for a truce. On 11 November an armistice was signed and the First World War was over.

Revision task

Make a copy of the table below. In column 2 use key words to summarise the part played by the British. In column 3 judge how important each event was for the outcome of the war on a scale of 1 to 5, with 5 being the most important. Give a brief explanation for each decision.

Event	Part played by British	Importance (1–5)
The BEF and 1914		
The Somme, 1916		
The events of 1918		

Exam practice

SOURCE B   A photograph of a German trench, 1 July 1916, during the Battle of the Somme.

1 Study Source B. What was the purpose of this representation? Use details from the photograph and your own knowledge to explain your answer. *(8 marks)*

Exam tip   The Exam practice question on the left is an example of a question 2 from Unit 3. You need to explain why this photograph was taken and printed. Note that it is a German trench and the scene of destruction was designed to show the success of the Allied attack on the first day of the Battle of the Somme. Use your own knowledge of these events in your answer.

7.3 The Home Front and social change, 1914–18

The powers of the Government increased during the First World War.

DORA

During the First World War, the Government imposed regulations and censorship that limited what people could do or say. The Defence of the Realm Act (DORA) was passed in August 1914. Its list of restrictions grew as the war went on.

DORA's measures were intended to provide for the efficient government of the country and to make sure that no help was given to the enemy. Measures included allowing the Government to take over any factory or workshop, to censor newspapers, to limit the hours pubs could open and even to water down beer.

> **Exam tip** You do not have to revise all of these measures. Make sure you know three or four.

Censorship and propaganda

To improve morale, newspapers were encouraged to print stories of British and Allied heroism and bravery, giving the impression that the war was being fought with huge successes. No pictures of dead soldiers were allowed to be printed. However, the long lists of official deaths and of missing soldiers increasingly showed how biased the reporting was.

Propaganda continued to be produced throughout the war – pamphlets, posters, newspaper reports and adverts. These gave the impression that the Germans were evil, and the British should be proud to participate in the German defeat. From the autumn of 1914, stories circulated about German atrocities in Belgium – women had been shot for no reason; babies had been bayoneted; nuns had been raped. Newspapers in France, Britain and the USA circulated the stories, and Belgian refugees added their own accounts. Whilst some civilians did suffer, the extent of the suffering was greatly exaggerated for propaganda purposes. The Germans were nicknamed 'Huns' – the name of a barbaric people who lived during the fourth to the fifth centuries AD. Many people wanted to believe that Germans of the early twentieth century were similarly cruel and evil.

Only later in the war did the Government begin to allow a more realistic picture to be presented. For example, it released an official film of the Battle of the Somme to be shown at cinemas. Some people fainted during its screening, even though it did not come anywhere near to showing the full extent of the horror.

> **Comment**
>
> *A significant proportion of men fought in 'Pals Battalions' where groups of friends were deliberately kept together. Whilst this was good for morale in the trenches, the effect back home was horrific when a battalion suffered heavy losses as close neighbours lost many friends and relations all at once.*

Recruitment and conscription

The War Minister, Lord Kitchener, planned to rely on volunteers to enlarge the army. There were 175,000 volunteer recruits by the end of September 1914, and from then on an average of 125,000 a month. There were many reasons why so many men were keen to join up. Some were motivated by patriotism, others because war seemed to promise adventure in an age when there were few opportunities to travel. Many were simply escaping from poverty and unemployment.

Men reluctant to join the armed forces were shamed into doing so. In London, some women handed out white feathers to any young man not in uniform. Public speakers whipped up enthusiasm in the crowd, with men encouraged to sign up there and then while influenced by the excitement of the moment.

However, as the war went on, there was a shortage of recruits. This was partly because there were not so many men eligible to volunteer, but it was also because the real horrors of war were becoming better understood. So in January 1916, the Government passed an act allowing all single men between the ages of 18 and 41 to be called up (conscripted) for active service. This was extended to all married men of the same age group later in the year.

> **Comment**
>
> *Other men were encouraged to stay at home – for example, coal miners and train drivers – as they were essential for maintaining basic services on the Home Front.*

Conscientious objectors

Some men, known as conscientious objectors, refused to join up because they thought it was wrong to fight and kill. The media and a good part of the public had little sympathy for such men – they were seen as cowards. Some conscientious objectors were prepared to work in the war effort in a non-fighting role (for example, as ambulance men) but others refused to have anything to do with the war, and were imprisoned on the assumption that they could be spies.

Rationing

At the beginning of the war there was a shortage of food as many people rushed to stockpile supplies. After this initial panic, supplied settled down for a while, helped by the measures taken by the Government under DORA. However, Britain relied on imports for much of its food, and German submarine operations effectively blocked much of this supply. The situation became acute in 1917 when German submarines successfully attacked supply ships crossing the Atlantic. In response, the Government tried to operate a voluntary rationing scheme, with limits on bread, meat and sugar. However, this was unsuccessful and the shortages continued.

Desperate attempts were made to grow more food. Grassed areas were turned into vegetable patches, as were public parks. In fact, over two and a half million acres of land were ploughed up for growing vegetables or keeping animals. Much of the work in the fields was undertaken by the new Women's Land Army because a large proportion of farm workers had volunteered to fight at the front.

In spite of all the Government's attempts to solve the food shortages, a limited form of rationing was introduced in 1918. Meat, sugar, butter, cheese and margarine had to be obtained with a ration card at the butcher's and grocer's shop with which a person was registered. Each person was allowed fifteen ounces (425 g) of meat per week, five ounces (140 g) of bacon and four ounces (110 g) of butter or margarine. This rationing system worked and food queues disappeared. It is also claimed that at the end of the war poorer people were healthier than they had been at the beginning of the war, partly as a result of getting a fairer share of healthy food through rationing.

> ## Revision task
> Draw a mind map to summarise government policies during the First World War, including DORA, censorship, propaganda, recruitment and rationing.

The part played by women

Before the war started, British women mostly accepted the role given to them – that is, to look after the home and bring up children.

In 1914, the war started to have a major impact on the position of women in British society, and on their attitude towards themselves. During the war about five million men joined the army. With so many men away fighting (and nearly one million not returning alive), there was a huge shortage of workers, especially in the jobs traditionally done by men. Women worked in the following areas:

- War work: in factories and steel mills; driving buses; building ships; or working in agriculture in the Women's Land Army.
- New war work: large numbers of women worked in munitions factories, making bullets and shells for ammunition. The number increased from 200,000 in 1914 to nearly one million in 1918. The work was highly dangerous; sometimes there were major explosions. The chemicals that women worked with tended to turn their skin yellow, and they were nicknamed 'canaries'. Industrial work was well paid. In munitions factories women could earn about £4 per week, compared with £2 a month as a domestic servant.
- The armed services: women were allowed to join up from April 1917 onwards. Most of the woman who entered the armed forces took over clerical and administrative duties normally done by men, releasing men to fight at the front.
- Nurses: about 23,000 women volunteered to serve as nurses close to the front line, often working in France or Belgium.
- Volunteer Aid Detachment: this provided cooks, kitchen maids, laundry workers and drivers.

The work done by many women affected their status. Many were receiving their own wage packet for the first time, making them financially independent. Some adapted their social behaviour and changed their style of dress, even daring to wear trousers. Others were more willing to go out on their own, even going into pubs, drinking alcohol and smoking in public.

During the war, the suffragettes suspended their campaign of violence and fully co-operated with the war effort. Increasingly, women were seen by men as sensible, and more capable of making decisions.

Women at the end of the war

The loyalty and service of women during the war was recognised by the all-male British Government. In 1918, the Representation of the People Act gave the vote to women over the age of 30. (Men could vote at the age of 21.) In 1919, women were allowed to do jury service, become lawyers and join the Civil Service. (Only in 1928 did women get the vote on the same terms as men.)

On the other hand, when the war ended, women were forced to give up many of the jobs they had taken over. It was thought to be only fair that returning soldiers were treated as heroes and given priority.

> **Exam tip** Remember to give a balanced answer if asked about the effects of the First World War on the position of women. They gained the vote and the confidence of doing 'men's jobs' but generally went back to their pre-war jobs and roles afterwards.

Revision task

Make a copy of the table on the right. Complete it with key words to show the changes to the position of women as a result of the First World War.

Women before the war	Women during the war	Women after the war

Exam practice

SOURCE C

A government poster issued in 1917.

SOURCE D

From a history textbook published in 2009.

'In early 1918, the government introduced compulsory rationing of sugar, butter, meat and beer. Every person had a book of coupons which had to be handed to the shopkeeper when rationed food was bought.'

1 Study Source C. What was the purpose of this representation? Use details from the poster and your own knowledge to explain your answer. *(8 marks)*

2 How reliable are Sources C and D as evidence of the methods used by the government to deal with food shortages? Explain your answer, using both sources and your own knowledge. *(10 marks)*

> **Exam tip: q1** Exam practice question 1 on the left is an example of a question 2 from Unit 3. You need to explain why this poster was put out by the government in 1917: what is it trying to make people think, or do? Refer to details from the source to support your answer. Use your own knowledge of the food situation in Britain in 1917 to explain your answer.

> **Exam tip: q2** Exam practice question 2 on the left is an example of a question 4 from Unit 3. You need to use your own knowledge to compare the reliability of *both* sources on the basis of:
> - what is in the sources, what each one says,
> - the nature, origin and purpose of each source.
>
> Reach a judgement about both sources by comparing the usefulness of each one in answering the question (government methods of dealing with food shortages).

7.4 Economic and social change, 1918–29

During the 1920s there were further changes in the role of women, whilst the Government had to deal with serious industrial unrest culminating in the General Strike of 1926.

The changing role of women, 1918–28

During the 1920s women did make some progress, especially in their political and social position. However, there was little or no change in employment opportunities.

Political progress

- There was some progress in the political position, with women aged 30 and over getting the vote in 1918. However, younger women, in their twenties, were disappointed with the age limit. They were considered too young and immature to cope in a responsible way with the vote. The real reason was that men feared a female majority of voters.
- Women also won the right to stand for Parliament and in 1919 Nancy Astor became the first woman MP to take her seat in Parliament. In 1928 women aged 21 and over were given the vote. At last they had equal voting rights to men.
- In 1929 Margaret Bondfield became the first female member of government.

Social progress

The war had given many women greater confidence and changed their attitude to their appearance and social habits.
- Young women no longer had chaperones. They were able to go to the cinema or to dances with boyfriends without having to take an aunt or other female with them.
- The flapper was the most extreme example of these social changes. These were young women, in their twenties, who challenged the old-fashioned ideas about women. They wore revealing clothes with short skirts, a lot of make-up and short hair. They drank and smoked in public and performed modern dances such as the Charleston.

Employment opportunities

After the First World War women returned to their traditional, unskilled, low paid jobs or their roles as housewives. By the 1930s women's wages were only half those of men, even if they were doing the same job.

However, there was some progress:
- The Sex Disqualification Removal Act of 1919 meant that women could no longer be barred from any job because of their sex. In theory, they could now enter professions such as law and architecture. However, the law still only applied to single women. Once married, a woman had to give up her job.
- In 1925 the Civil Service admitted women to government service for the first time.

Revision tasks

1 Make a copy of the set of scales shown here. Use key words to make notes on each pan indicating progress, and lack of progress, for women.

2 Overall do you think women made progress in the 1920s? Explain your answer.

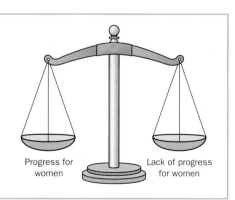

Progress for women | Lack of progress for women

Exam tip Answers on the progress of women are often generalised and vague. Remember to revise key developments such as the Sex Disqualification Removal Act. This will impress an examiner.

Industrial unrest, 1918–26

In 1926, there was a general strike which lasted for nine days. This was due to problems in the coal industry and developments in the trade union movement.

Problems in the coal industry

During the First World War, the Government nationalised, or took over, the coal mines. This benefited the miners because they got:

- a seven-hour day
- a national minimum wage (the same wages for every miner, no matter which pit he worked in).

Coal mining, however, suffered in the years after the First World War.

- Exports of British coal, which before the war had been 100 million tons a year, fell as British coal had to compete with the cheaper coal produced by countries such as the USA, Germany and Poland.
- The miners wanted the Government to permanently nationalise the coal industry. In 1919, the Prime Minister, Lloyd George, set up the Sankey Commission to look into the coal industry and promised to accept its findings. In 1920, it recommended permanent nationalisation. Lloyd George went back on his word and would not accept this conclusion.
- When the coal industry faced a serious slump in the winter of 1920–21 and began to lose five million pounds a month, the Government handed the industry back to private owners. Their solution was to cut the miners' pay and make them work a longer day.

The trade union movement

The trade union movement grew larger and stronger in the years before and after the First World War.

Some trade unions at this time believed that strike action was the most effective way of bringing about changes in society. Their ultimate weapon was 'direct action', or strikes culminating in a national or general strike. The British trade unions moved closer to this idea with the formation of the Triple Industrial Alliance in 1913.

- The three largest unions, the Miners' Federation of Great Britain (MFGB), the Transport Workers' Federation (mainly dockworkers) and the National Union of Railwaymen, agreed that if one member came out on strike the other two would come out in sympathy.
- This would effectively lead to a general strike as the country would be paralysed.

The Triple Alliance was abandoned during the First World War but trade unions increased their strength as membership doubled from four to eight million between 1914 and 1920. There was a great number of strikes in the period 1919–20 and the Triple Alliance was revived in February 1919.

> **Exam tip** Remember that the General Strike was not just caused by problems in the coal industry. Industrial militancy and the Triple Alliance also played their part.

Black Friday, 15 April 1921

There was almost a general strike in 1921.

- In April 1921, the coal industry owners announced wage cuts and a longer working day. They locked out the miners until they agreed to these terms. The longer working day did not make sense. It meant that miners would produce even more coal that could not be sold.
- The MFGB called upon the transport workers and the railwaymen to support them in a strike against the wage cut on Friday 15 April.
- At the very last moment, however, these two unions pulled out, leaving the miners to fight on alone. That is why the miners called it 'Black Friday'.
- The Triple Alliance, which was now known at the 'Cripple Alliance', collapsed. The miners were eventually starved back to work in July 1921. They had to accept pay cuts and the addition of an extra 30 minutes to the working day.

Red Friday, 31 July 1925

Coal prices continued to fall, leading to the second occasion when there could have been a general strike.

- The pit owners again announced a longer working day and pay cuts. The miners' leader, A. J. Cook, was furious. His reply, 'Not a penny off the pay! Not a minute on the day!' became the miners' slogan.
- The Trades Union Congress (TUC) backed the miners. All movement of coal by land or water was to be stopped from 31 July.
- The Conservative Prime Minister, Stanley Baldwin, was not ready for a general strike. He therefore gave a subsidy, or financial support, to the coal owners to last nine months and to prevent a cut in wages. In the meantime, he set up another commission, led by the Liberal Herbert Samuel, to study the problems in the coal industry and come up with a long-term solution.
- The unions called their success 'Red Friday'. It was, however, only a breathing space. Everyone knew there would be a showdown if the miners and pit owners did not agree about what was to happen when the Government subsidy ended on 1 May 1926.
- Meanwhile, the Government made preparations for a general strike.

The immediate cause of the strike

The Samuel Commission reported in March 1926 but failed to find a solution that would keep either side happy.

Shortly after the commission reported, Baldwin announced that the subsidy would end on 30 April. The owners then set wages even lower than they had previously proposed. The miners refused to accept this and were again locked out. They called on the other unions to support them by coming out on strike. The TUC agreed to support the miners and to negotiate with the Government on their behalf.

On 30 April 1926, the employers made their final offer –a thirteen per cent wage cut and a 'temporary' increase in the working day by one hour. It was rejected by the MFGB. On the following day, the TUC voted by a large majority in favour of striking in support of the miners. Talks between the TUC and Baldwin continued in an effort to find a solution. These were called off by Baldwin on 2 May when he heard that the printers at the offices of the *Daily Mail* had refused to print an article, 'For King and Country', which criticised the miners. The strike began at midnight on 3 May.

Exam tip The miners were locked out in April 1926. The other unions then came out on strike in sympathy with the miners.

The General Strike of 1926

This lasted for nine days and brought much of the country to a standstill.

At first, the strike seemed successful and in the first few days the number of strikers actually increased. The strikers were well organised. They allowed essential supplies and had no intention of bringing out hospital workers or other key workers. There was little trouble and only one person was killed in the first week. However, scenes of violence gradually increased. In Glasgow and Doncaster strikers were arrested, tried and imprisoned. There were police baton charges, stone throwing, attempted derailment of trains driven by volunteers and overturned lorries and buses.

Much to the surprise of the miners and most strikers, the TUC did not extend the strike. Instead, on 12 May its leaders went to Downing Street and called off the strike.

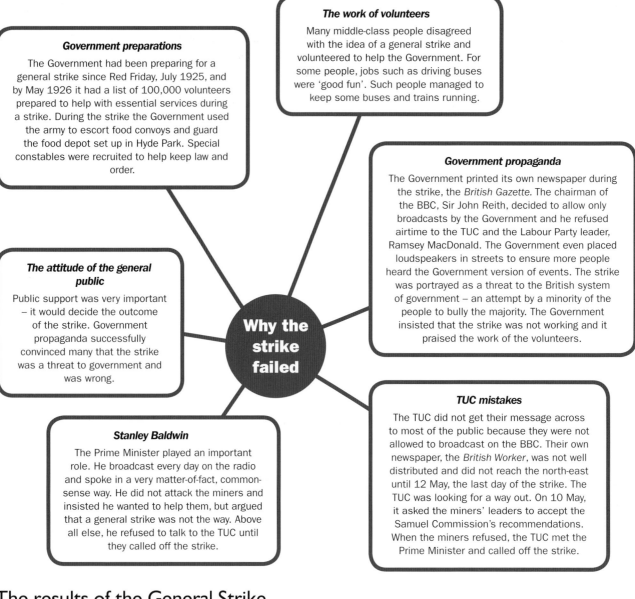

The work of volunteers

Many middle-class people disagreed with the idea of a general strike and volunteered to help the Government. For some people, jobs such as driving buses were 'good fun'. Such people managed to keep some buses and trains running.

Government preparations

The Government had been preparing for a general strike since Red Friday, July 1925, and by May 1926 it had a list of 100,000 volunteers prepared to help with essential services during a strike. During the strike the Government used the army to escort food convoys and guard the food depot set up in Hyde Park. Special constables were recruited to help keep law and order.

Government propaganda

The Government printed its own newspaper during the strike, the *British Gazette*. The chairman of the BBC, Sir John Reith, decided to allow only broadcasts by the Government and he refused airtime to the TUC and the Labour Party leader, Ramsey MacDonald. The Government even placed loudspeakers in streets to ensure more people heard the Government version of events. The strike was portrayed as a threat to the British system of government – an attempt by a minority of the people to bully the majority. The Government insisted that the strike was not working and it praised the work of the volunteers.

The attitude of the general public

Public support was very important – it would decide the outcome of the strike. Government propaganda successfully convinced many that the strike was a threat to government and was wrong.

Why the strike failed

Stanley Baldwin

The Prime Minister played an important role. He broadcast every day on the radio and spoke in a very matter-of-fact, common-sense way. He did not attack the miners and insisted he wanted to help them, but argued that a general strike was not the way. Above all else, he refused to talk to the TUC until they called off the strike.

TUC mistakes

The TUC did not get their message across to most of the public because they were not allowed to broadcast on the BBC. Their own newspaper, the *British Worker*, was not well distributed and did not reach the north-east until 12 May, the last day of the strike. The TUC was looking for a way out. On 10 May, it asked the miners' leaders to accept the Samuel Commission's recommendations. When the miners refused, the TUC met the Prime Minister and called off the strike.

The results of the General Strike

- The miners were left to fight on alone. Some began to drift back to work in August 1926 and the majority had returned by December. They had to accept the pay cut and the longer working day. The problems of the coal industry had not been solved. Indeed, they were now even worse due to the exports lost during the strike.
- Calling off the General Strike lowered confidence in the TUC. Many workers were penalised when they returned to work. Ringleaders were sacked and others had to accept inferior terms of employment. Baldwin passed the Trades Disputes Act in 1927 to make all future general strikes illegal. Workers could no longer come out on strike in sympathy with other workers.
- The General Strike was a disaster for the trade union movement. TUC membership fell from 5.5 million in 1925 to 3.75 million in 1930. Nevertheless, it was a success for the Labour Party. Many workers now turned away from strike action and began to support the idea of a Labour government to improve their living and working conditions. In 1929, the Labour Party, for the first time, won more seats than either the Liberals or Conservatives.

> **Revision tasks**
>
> 1 Draw a timeline of the events of 1918–26 that led to the General Strike.
>
> 2 Use key words to explain the effects that the failure of the strike had on:
> - the miners
> - the coal industry
> - the trade union movement
> - the Labour Party.

Revision tasks

3 Make a copy of the table below. Make a decision on the importance of each factor in bringing about the failure of the strike. Use information from pages 82–84 to explain your decisions. An example has been done for you.

	Decisive	Important	Quite important
Government preparations			
The work of volunteers			
Government propaganda	This was decisive because it convinced the general public that the strike was wrong.		
Stanley Baldwin			
TUC mistakes			

Exam tip The Exam practice question on the right is an example of a question 5 from Unit 3. You need to:
- use Source E, other sources and your own knowledge to agree with the statement
- then use other sources and your own knowledge to disagree with the statement
- comment on the reliability of each source in order to judge the strength or weakness of each side of the argument
- reach a balanced judgement on the interpretation.

Exam practice

SOURCE E

An extract from Baldwin's radio broadcast of 6 May.

'Constitutional government is being attacked. The laws of England are people's birthright. These laws are in your keeping. You have made Parliament their guardian. The General Strike is a challenge to Parliament, and is the road to ruin.'

1 Source E suggests that the General Strike was an attack on the British constitution. How far do you agree with this interpretation? Use your own knowledge, Source E and any other sources from other textbooks which you find helpful to explain your answer. *(16 marks)*

Key content

You need to have a good working knowledge of the following areas.
Tick off each item once you are confident in your knowledge.

- [ ] the methods and activities of the WSPU, WFL and NUWSS
- [ ] the reaction of the Liberal Government to the women's suffrage movement
- [ ] child welfare measures, OAPs and insurance against sickness and unemployment
- [ ] the role of the BEF in 1914
- [ ] the part played by the British on the Western Front, 1915–17, especially the Battle of the Somme
- [ ] the trench system, trench warfare and new weapons
- [ ] the part played by the British in the defeat of Germany in 1918
- [ ] the role of DORA, censorship and propaganda
- [ ] recruitment and rationing
- [ ] the impact of the First World War on the position of women
- [ ] changes in the position of women in the 1920s
- [ ] the industrial unrest in the years 1918–26
- [ ] the problems of the coal industry after the First World War
- [ ] the reasons for the failure of the General Strike
- [ ] the effects of the General Strike on the coal industry and the trade union movement.

Check your knowledge online with our Quick quizzes at www.hodderplus.co.uk/modernworldhistory.

Chapter 8: War and the transformation of British society c.1931–51

During this period Britain experienced a major economic depression and became involved in the Second World War. In the years after 1945 the Labour Government introduced important changes which created the welfare state.

Key topics

These are the key topics you need to revise. As with all examination topics you first need to learn the content so you know it well enough to answer a range of questions on this topic.

- the impact of the Depression, 1931–39
- Britain alone
- Britain at war
- Labour in power, 1945–51.

8.1 The impact of the Depression, 1931–39

The Wall Street Crash in the USA in 1929 (see Chapter 6) led to a worldwide depression. Indeed, Britain followed the USA into depression with the decline of its traditional heavy industries – coal, iron and steel, cotton and shipbuilding.

Unemployment and the government response

Unemployment reached a peak of nearly 3 million by 1933 but varied considerably from area to area.

'Depressed' Britain

In 1931, the national unemployment rate was 23 per cent, but this figure hid the real effects of the Depression. By the mid-1930s, the worst hit areas, such as Jarrow on Tyneside and Merthyr Tydfil in south Wales, had over 60 per cent unemployment. In Oxford it was less than 6 per cent.

In Jarrow, the local coal mine, Hebburn Colliery, closed in 1930. In the following year, the steel works closed. In 1934, National Shipbuilders' Security Ltd, an organisation set up to close shipyards which were not profitable, shut down Palmer's, the shipyard in Jarrow. This had a devastating effect on the town. Ellen Wilkinson, the local Labour MP, described it as 'the town that was murdered'.

The government response

There is much debate on government action. Did it do enough to help the 'depressed areas' and the unemployed? In 1931, a National Government was set up to reduce unemployment. This was a coalition of the three main parties – Conservatives, Liberals and Labour.

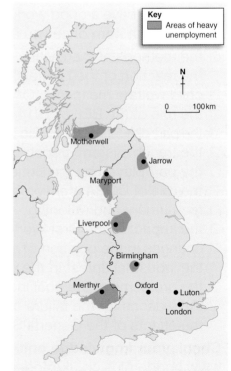

Key
Areas of heavy unemployment

Unemployment in Britain in the 1930s.

- *Unemployment benefit*. For those out of work, there was unemployment benefit (or dole money). Between 1929 and 1931, the numbers of unemployed grew rapidly. The Government found it was paying far more out in benefits than it was receiving in taxes. As a consequence, the National Government cut unemployment benefit by 10 per cent in 1931. It also introduced the means test.
- *The means test, 1931*. Many people claimed that the means test was more about the Government trying to save money than helping the unemployed. It was carried out by officials from the local authorities' Public Assistance Committees (PACs), which had been set up in 1930. The unemployed who were claiming benefit had to reveal what everyone in their house, including grown-up children, had in savings and earnings. The test even looked at the value of things in the home that could be sold to raise money. The means test was extremely unpopular.
  - It was humiliating for families to have to reveal earnings, savings and the value of things they owned.
  - If the officials thought there was enough money in the house, they would stop the dole.
  - Some local authorities applied the means test very harshly. Others, such as those in County Durham, refused to carry it out.
  - The test created great strain in families, especially if one of the older children who had a job was forced to pay more towards the family funds.
- *Import Duties Act, 1932*. The Government tried to protect British industry by increasing the price of foreign goods. The idea was that if more British goods were bought, more would have to be produced, and so more people would be employed to produce them. The Import Duties Act benefited British car and electrical goods industries in the south of England but had little effect in areas of high unemployment. Moreover, other countries put taxes on goods coming into their country from Britain. This made it more difficult for British export industries.
- *Special Areas Act, 1934*. The Government realised that certain parts of the country were suffering far more than others from the Depression. It decided to give additional help to these 'special' areas. The Special Areas Act appointed two commissioners with a budget of 2 million pounds to try to attract some of the new industries to the old industrial areas. The initiative had limited success. Some industrial estates were established, such as the Team Valley Trading Estate in Gateshead, but it created fewer than 15,000 jobs. Many companies did not want to move to the north of England. Small industrial estates could not replace the coal mining or shipbuilding industries.

Exam tip Remember to give a balanced view of government measures. Some helped and some hindered the plight of the unemployed.

How effective were these measures?

By the end of the 1930s unemployment had fallen to 1 million. This was due partly to government policies and partly to favourable circumstances such as a revival in world trade, which helped Britain's exports. It was also due to rearmament, which greatly helped the traditional industries, especially coal, iron and steel, and shipbuilding.

The experience of the unemployed

In an area of high unemployment, everyone in the community felt the impact when jobs were lost. Local shopkeepers were hit hard. Shops closed, with the shopkeepers joining the ranks of the unemployed.

Effects of unemployment

- **Poverty**. Several surveys of the 1930s showed the connection between unemployment and poverty. In 1936, Seebohm Rowntree did a survey of

Comment

Some historians have argued that the measures undertaken by the National Government actually made the situation worse. They point to the means test and Import Duties Act as examples. The latter encouraged other countries to put duties on British goods and made it more difficult to export.

poverty in York and found that 72.6 per cent of unemployed workers lived below the poverty line.

- **Health**. Not surprisingly, the health of the unemployed and their families, especially children, suffered. Several studies showed that the unemployed had an inadequate diet. They ate a lot of bread, margarine, potatoes, sugar and tea, but little meat, fresh fruit and vegetables, and milk.

- **Psychological**. One common consequence of unemployment was poor mental health. Investigators found a general trend. The first week or so of unemployment was treated as a holiday. People got up early, put on their best clothes and went down to their local labour exchange seeking work. After a few weeks, confidence began to decline, expectations fell and the unemployed took less interest in personal appearance. Many people, used to being the breadwinner of the family, felt guilty and lost all self-respect and self-esteem.

Revision tasks

1 Make a copy of the table below. Use the information on pages 86–87 and above to explain each measure and whether it helped or hindered Britain's economic position.

Measure	Explanation	Help	Hinder
Unemployment benefit			
Means test			
Import Duties Act			
Special Areas Act			

2 What effects did the Depression have on the standard of living of the unemployed?

The Jarrow Crusade

This is one of the most famous events of the 1930s.

Reasons for marching

Palmer's shipyard in Jarrow began to decline after the First World War. There were fewer warships being built and after 1929 fewer and fewer cargo ships. In the early 1930s orders dried up completely. Unemployment rose from 3,245 in 1929 to 7,178 in 1933.

The end came in 1934. A group of shipyard owners set up National Shipbuilders' Security Ltd (see page 86). They decided to buy up smaller yards and then scrap them. Palmer's was one of the first to go. In 1934 it was bought up and the yard was closed. It was announced that no ships would be built there for 40 years. This had a terrible effect on Jarrow. Unemployment reached 80 per cent at one point.

The march

The people of Jarrow decided to fight back. Public meetings were held and the town council decided to draw up a petition demanding the right to work. It organised a march to London to present the petition to the Government. Two hundred men were carefully selected by the local officer of health for the long journey to London. The men decided to march between 15 and 25 miles per day.

There had been a number of hunger marches previously, but the Jarrow march caught the public imagination. It had been approved by the local council and the marchers were led on their journey by Ellen Wilkinson MP. Each night the marchers were accommodated along the route by householders who supported their cause. The press gave the protestors mouth organs so they could march to music.

Comment

Palmer's also suffered from another problem. By the 1930s the yard was too small for the type of ship that was being built. The Queen Elizabeth *and* Queen Mary*, which were launched in the 1930s, were over 80,000 tonnes. Palmer's could not cope with ships that size.*

What it achieved

- It publicised the plight of towns like Jarrow to people in the more prosperous south of England.
- The police praised the marchers for being well organised and disciplined.
- The men returned home as heroes.
- A few men found work in the Team Valley Trading Estate in nearby Gateshead.

However:
- The Government refused to let them present the petition when they got to London.
- They did not get new work for the town.
- When they returned to Jarrow, they discovered that their unemployment benefit had been stopped as they had not been available for work while on the march.

Revision tasks

1 Make a copy of the set of scales shown here. Use key words to complete each side of the scales.

2 Was the Jarrow march a success? Explain your answer.

Achievements of the Jarrow march — Failures of the Jarrow march

Exam practice

SOURCE A

From *Love on the Dole*, a novel written by Walter Greenwood in the 1930s.

'It got to you slowly like a malignant disease. You fell into the habit of slouching, of putting your hands in your pockets and keeping them there. Of glancing at people secretly, ashamed of your secret. You prayed for the winter evenings and the kindly darkness. Pants with the backside patched and re-patched; patches on knees, on elbows. Jesus! All bloody patches.'

1 What can you learn from Source A about the effects of unemployment? *(6 marks)*

Exam tip The Exam practice question on the left is an example of a question 1 from Unit 3. You need to find at least two things that the source tells you (these are called inferences). Back up each one with selected words from the source.

8.2 Britain alone

Britain entered the Second World War in September 1939. By June 1940 France had been defeated and Britain alone faced Germany and Italy from 1940 to 1941 until the German invasion of the USSR.

The British Expeditionary Force, Dunkirk and Churchill

Hitler's armies invaded and defeated Poland in September 1939.

The British Expeditionary Force

From the end of September 1939 to April 1940, little progress was made in the war in the west. This became known as the 'Phoney War' (or pretend war) in Britain and the *Sitzkrieg*, or sitting war, in Germany.

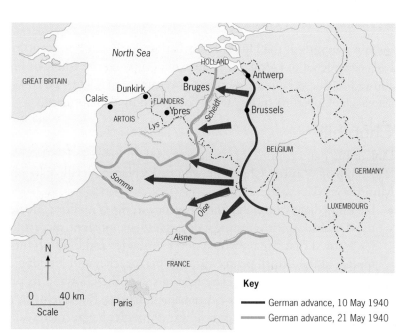

The German advance through Belgium and France, May 1940.

The defeat of France

On 13 May 1940, the Germans launched a *Blitzkrieg* attack against the Low Countries (Belgium and the Netherlands) and France. It was an outstanding success. German attacks rolled swiftly across the Netherlands and Belgium. Dutch attempts to delay the German advances by opening the dykes and flooding the land were too little too late. The Germans used glider planes to land behind the Belgian lines of defences and outflank their defenders. The Netherlands surrendered within five days.

Other troops attacked the French. The French High Command was sure that the expensive line of underground forts on the **Maginot Line** would stop any German attack. The Germans, however, decided not to attack this line – *Blitzkrieg* avoided enemy strongpoints. Instead the Germans attacked the weakest part of the French defences, the Ardennes. This was a heavily wooded area, which seemed unsuitable for tanks. To the astonishment of the French, the Germans attacked this area and broke through to Sedan.

French resistance crumbled as the German tanks raced through to the Channel coast, where they planned to cut off the retreat of the 200,000-strong BEF. By the tenth day, the Germans had reached the Channel. Eight days later, Belgium surrendered.

Dunkirk

British and French troops retreated to Dunkirk where they awaited either evacuation or capture. For reasons that are not quite clear, Hitler ordered the advancing German troops to stop. This gave the Allies a breathing space in which to carry out an evacuation. Between 26 May and 4 June 198,000 British and 140,000 French and Belgian troops were evacuated.

Dunkirk was celebrated in Britain as a great achievement.
- The RAF outfought the Luftwaffe (the German air force) over the beaches of Dunkirk. It was a great success for the British navy.
- Many troops were rescued to fight another day.
- The 'Dunkirk spirit' was born. Winston Churchill, the Prime Minister, made the British determined to fight against Hitler.

However, in many respects it was a disaster.
- Around 300,000 troops were left behind and forced to surrender.
- Most of the army's equipment had to be abandoned.
- France was left to fight alone and soon surrendered.

Within a month of the Dunkirk evacuation, Paris had been captured and France had surrendered to Germany. Instead of occupying the whole of France, Germany allowed southern France to set up a government at Vichy run by General Petain. The Vichy Government was really controlled by the Germans.

Churchill

One of the main reasons for British survival in the years 1940–41 was the leadership of Winston Churchill, who had replaced Neville Chamberlain as Prime Minister in May 1940.
- He immediately brought a new urgency to the war effort. He helped to create the 'Dunkirk spirit', turning a defeat into an apparent success for the British. He insisted that Britain would never surrender and built up the confidence and morale of the British people through his speeches and 'bulldog' approach.
- Churchill also cultivated close relations with the USA and its president, Roosevelt. Although the USA remained neutral, Roosevelt was prepared to supply Britain with the needs of war, through an agreement called 'Lend Lease'. These supplies proved vital during this difficult period.

Key term

Maginot Line: a line of fortifications along the north east frontier of France.

Comment

Churchill portrayed Dunkirk as a great British victory due to the evacuation of so many troops. This was, in most respects, government propaganda to keep up the morale of the British people.

Exam tip Ensure you give a balanced view of Dunkirk.

Comment

Churchill and the spirit of the British people are rightly praised for Britain's survival alone against Germany between 1940 and 1941. Yet Britain's survival was also due to favourable circumstances, such as Hitler's decision not to use tanks at Dunkirk, Roosevelt's willingness to agree to Lend Lease and, most important of all, Hitler's decision to invade the Soviet Union in June 1941.

Revision task

Make a copy of the table below. Use information from pages 89–90 to give your verdict on Dunkirk – success or disaster.

Success	Disaster

The Battle of Britain

One of the most important reasons for British survival in the war was the defeat of the German air force during the Battle of Britain.

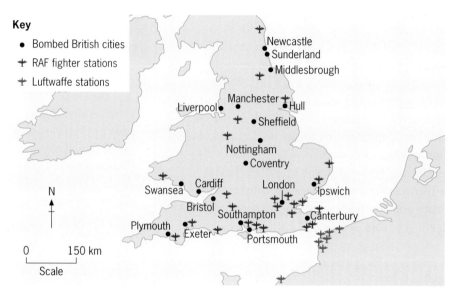

The Battle of Britain.

Britain would not have survived without the RAF and its successes in the Battle of Britain. Hitler planned to attack Britain but first he needed to destroy the RAF and gain control of the skies over Britain. The first attacks by the German Luftwaffe were on shipping in the English Channel and the ports on the south coast. These were followed by bombing raids on radar stations and then airfields. Finally, from mid-August, came the attacks on Fighter Command. By the first week in September the Luftwaffe were getting the upper hand as the RAF ran out of reserves of pilots and planes. Fortunately Hitler diverted the Luftwaffe to attacks on London. When daylight raids were renewed on 15 September, the RAF regained the initiative.

The RAF was successful for several reasons:
- German mistakes – Hitler made the mistake of diverting the Luftwaffe from attacks on the RAF to bombing London.
- German weaknesses – the German bombers were often not escorted by fighter planes. They became easy targets for the RAF fighters.
- The British had superior fighter planes – the Spitfire and the Hurricane.
- Since the mid-1930s the British had devised an early warning system using radar which meant they knew when and where the Germans would attack. RAF fighter planes were in the air and ready when the German bombers and fighters appeared.

The Blitz

This was the name given to German attempts to bomb Britain out of the war.

German bombing

The Luftwaffe's bombing of British towns and cities became known as the 'Blitz'. Hitler hoped that the Blitz would force Britain to surrender and that the German people would enjoy revenge for the bombing that they had suffered. (On 25 August 1940, Britain had begun the night-bombing of German towns and cities.) From 7 September until 2 November 1940, London was bombed every night. Bombs landed on London Zoo and the papers reported that 'the morale of the monkeys remained unaffected'. The House of Commons building was destroyed and the Commons had to move into the House of Lords. Buckingham Palace was damaged but King George VI was often on the scene after a severe raid to encourage people as they struggled to save those trapped under the debris.

The German bombing raids continued until well into 1941, when most of the Luftwaffe was needed on the Eastern Front. London was not the only city to suffer. The Germans also attacked other towns and cities such as Hull, Plymouth, Bristol, Liverpool, Manchester and Birmingham. The most famous of these attacks was the raid on Coventry. On the night of 14 November 1940, much of the city, including the cathedral, was destroyed. Yet in spite of this savage raid, the factories in Coventry were back in full production within five days.

Other smaller towns and cities were hit in 1941–42 in the so-called Baedeker raids. The targets were chosen by the Germans from the Baedeker tourist guide book. The cathedral cities of Canterbury and Norwich were among those hit.

There were further air attacks in 1944–45 from V-1 and V-2 missiles, based in northern France.

- Six thousand V-1 bombs reached targets in Britain, causing 20,000 casualties and considerable damage to houses.
- Around 500 V-2s hit London between September 1944 and March 1945, causing 9,000 casualties.

Air raid precautions

The Government supplied its citizens with air raid shelters.

- The first shelters were delivered in February 1939. These were Anderson shelters, which were sunk into the ground in people's gardens. They had enough room for a family and were safer than staying in a house.
- Later, in 1941, the Morrison shelter was introduced, which could be erected indoors. By the end of the year 500,000 of these shelters had been distributed.

When the raids first began, people in London were not allowed to use the underground railway stations for fear they would get trapped. But public pressure forced the authorities to give way and they became popular places to shelter.

The 'blackout' had the most immediate effect on the British people. In order that German bombers would not see cities from the air, and therefore target their bombing more precisely, people had to ensure that no light was visible from their homes. Failure to do so meant a visit from the Air Raid Warden. Streetlights were not lit and cars had to drive without lights. This led to many accidents. In December 1939, over 1,500 people were killed on British roads. This was nearly three times the pre-war average of 600 deaths per month.

Evacuation

The Government expected that the Germans would attack Britain from the air so it took precautions to protect its civilians from bombings and gas attacks. Children were protected by being moved (evacuated) from the likeliest targets, the cities, into the countryside. The first evacuation was announced on 31 August 1939, the day before Hitler invaded Poland.

Many parents were reluctant to be separated from their children but did accept that they would be safer. Parents were told what the children needed to take with them and where they were to assemble for evacuation. The evacuation began on 1 September 1939. Many city schools were closed and many teachers went with the children to the countryside to continue teaching them.

At their destinations, the evacuees gathered in village or school halls where they were chosen by the foster family they were to live with. Homesickness and the 'Phoney War' (see page 89) saw many children drift back to the cities by Christmas 1939. When German planes started bombing London in 1940, a second evacuation from the cities took place, although not on the scale of the evacuation of 1939.

Successes of evacuation	Criticisms of evacuation
● Some children were very happy. They helped on farms and had far better diets than they had done before. ● Thousands were moved to the safety of the countryside and away from the bombing. ● In the long term, evacuation encouraged further social reform as it highlighted the poor condition of many children from the inner cities. ● It enabled mothers to take on vital war work.	● Many mothers and children returned to their homes during the 'Phoney War' and had to be evacuated again. ● The administration of evacuees was often chaotic with a mismatch in numbers of evacuees and foster homes. ● Some children had a miserable time. They were resented as a burden by their foster families, and they missed their own families, far away in the cities. ● Many country families were shocked by the evacuees they looked after. They had to deal with children who wet their beds and had no experience of using a knife and fork.

Revision tasks

1 Make a copy of these concentric circles. Write a reason in each circle for British success in the Battle of Britain, beginning with the most important in the middle. Use key words to explain your decisions.

2 Complete a table, listing the successes and failures of the Blitz from the German point of view.

3 Use key words to explain how the following were affected by evacuation:
- mothers
- children
- country families.

Exam practice

SOURCE C   A British poster from 1940.

"NEVER WAS SO MUCH OWED BY SO MANY TO SO FEW" *THE PRIME MINISTER*

1 Study Source C. What was the purpose of this representation? Use details of the poster and your own knowledge to explain your answer. *(8 marks)*

Exam tip The Exam practice question on the left is an example of a question 2 from Unit 3. You need to:
- explain what the message of the poster is
- use your own knowledge of the context to explain why it was put out at that time.

8.3 Britain at war

The role of the Government and women changed during the Second World War.

The role of government

The Government was responsible for propaganda and censorship as well as introducing rationing due to food shortages.

Propaganda

The Ministry of Information was responsible for propaganda and censorship. It monitored public opinion through an organisation called Mass Observation, which carried out surveys and reported on conversations in shops and pubs.

Propaganda was used in several ways.

- Poster campaigns encouraged people to join the voluntary services and work hard in order to help the war effort.
- Posters also warned people of the dangers of 'careless talk'. There was a fear that German spies could be working in the country so people were told not to discuss the war in public.
- Posters encouraged people to save for the war effort and not to waste food and other resources. The 'squander bug' became a regular feature of messages to housewives.

Censorship

Newspapers were censored by the Government during the war. They reported on the bombings but in an attempt to keep up morale they concentrated on the heroism of the rescuers rather than the deaths and injuries. The Government banned the publication of the *Daily Worker* newspaper in 1941 when it claimed that the war was being fought for the benefit of the bosses.

Rationing

At the outbreak of war, Britain grew only enough food to feed about one person in every three. Much food was imported but, as with the First World War, these imports were threatened by the activities of the German U-boats.

The Government introduced a series of measures to ensure there was an adequate supply of food. Rationing was introduced as early as January 1940. Each person had a ration book filled with coupons, which they used to buy the amount of food they were entitled to each week. Later, a points system was introduced, to give people greater choice in what they could buy. The Board of Trade also issued recipes showing people how to make healthy meals using food that was available.

At first, only butter, bacon and sugar were rationed. Later, this was extended to include tea and most basic foodstuffs, although vegetables were never rationed. People were asked to grow their own food so that less food would have to be imported. Window boxes, lawns, public parks and golf courses were used to grow vegetables to keep the nation fed and healthy.

> ## Revision tasks
>
> 1 Why was it necessary to introduce rationing?
>
> 2 Draw a spider diagram to show government measures in connection with rationing.

The changing role of women

Women's work

Industry was short of workers as men were conscripted. At first, women volunteered to fill vacant jobs. By 1941, industry was so short of workers that unmarried women were conscripted. Within two years, 57 per cent of workers were female. By 1943, nine out of ten single women were doing war work, and so were many married women. Some worked in industry, and those who worked in dangerous conditions, such as in the munitions industry, were well paid. Men were usually better paid for doing the same jobs but, even so, women were earning a lot more than before the war.

There was a similar shortage of workers on the land. About 80,000 women joined the Women's Land Army. They were given lodgings in remote areas, sometimes with very basic conditions. Many women travelled the country doing everyday farm jobs, such as haymaking, ploughing, harvesting and looking after animals.

Women in the armed forces

Women who were conscripted after 1941 could choose to join one of three organisations:
- the Auxiliary Territorial Service (ATS)
- the Women's Auxiliary Air Force (WAAF)
- the Women's Royal Naval Service (WRNS).

These forces were involved in providing support services rather than fighting, but they worked alongside men and faced the same dangers. Women operated searchlights or acted as radar controllers. Women pilots were also used to transfer planes from the factories to the airfields.

Effects on women

Life for many women had been very strict during the 1930s, but in wartime, there was a shortage of younger men at home, and there tended to be more freedom in sexual relationships. Some women argued that with all the dangers and worries of wartime they should be allowed to enjoy themselves.

But equality was still far off. For example, the Government would not commit itself to equal pay for women. An Equal Pay Commission was set up in 1943 and reported in 1946, but it had no powers to make recommendations. Similarly, the Ministry of Health refused to set up nurseries to provide childcare for working women, arguing that female employment was only for the duration of the war. By 1944 there were, however, 1,450 nurseries compared to 104 before the war. These were closed down after the war to force married women to give up their jobs and return to the home.

When the war ended, fewer women wanted to work. Many saw work as a wartime emergency and believed that their proper place was in the home. Many had delayed having children because of the war and now wanted to start families. The war did, however, bring some changes in attitudes towards married women working. In the 1950s, some of these women did find work when their children were growing up.

Comment

By 1944, there were 450,000 women working in these three armed services. Many women worked as mechanics, welders, carpenters and even gunners on anti-aircraft guns. However, traditional attitudes towards women remained. Most women in the services worked as cooks, cleaners or secretaries.

Comment

Women played a very important role on the Home Front but, as with the First World War, made limited gains in terms of job opportunities and their social position. After the war, most were expected to give up their jobs and return to their pre-war employment or settle for marriage and the roles of mother and housewife.

Exam practice

SOURCE D

A poster issued by the British Government during the Second World War.

SOURCE E

From a booklet put out to US soldiers coming to Britain in 1942.

'British women have proved themselves in this war. They have stuck to their posts near burning ammunition dumps. Delivered messages on foot after their motorcycles have been blasted from under them. They have pulled airmen from blazing planes ... So when you see a girl with a medal ribbon on her tunic she didn't get it for knitting more socks than anyone else in Ipswich.'

1 How reliable are Sources D and E as evidence of the contribution of women during the Second World War? Explain your answer, using Sources D and E and your own knowledge.   *(10 marks)*

Exam tip The Exam practice question on the left is an example of a question 4 from Unit 3. You need to use your own knowledge to compare the reliability of *both* sources on the basis of:
- what is in the sources, what each one shows or says
- the nature, origin and purpose of each source.

Reach a judgement about both sources by comparing the usefulness of each one in answering the question (women's contribution to the war).

D-Day and the defeat of Germany

The British played an important role in the D-Day invasions of 1944 and the eventual defeat of Germany.

D-Day

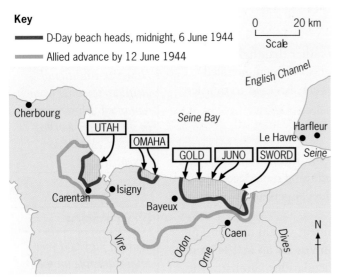

D-Day landings, June 1944.

On 6 June 1944 Allied forces landed on the beaches of Normandy in France and began the campaign to liberate western Europe from German occupation. The British and Canadian forces landed on beaches codenamed Sword, Juno and Gold and the US forces landed at Omaha and Utah. The Allies were quickly able to establish a beachhead (or fortified position) and, although pinned down in Normandy for almost a month, they eventually broke out and reached Paris within six weeks.

The success of D-Day was due to a combination of factors:

- The Allies had prepared very thoroughly for the invasion. Churchill delayed the assault until he felt the time was right. Allied troops were trained in landing tactics and new devices were developed to assist in the landings. These included artificial piers and harbours and an oil pipeline across the Channel.
- The Germans did not know where the landings would take place. Indeed, Allied bombing of the Calais area convinced Hitler that this would be the location. Even on the day of the invasion, he thought the landings in Normandy were a decoy and was slow to send reinforcements.
- The Allies had control of the air over the Channel and northern France. Ten thousand Allied planes escorted the invasion fleet and had also prepared the way by bombing communications to Normandy and carrying paratroopers behind German lines. The invasion fleet was the biggest ever assembled.
- Hitler refused to allow Field Marshal Rommel to take control of the Panzer tank divisions in Normandy. This weakened the German army when it tried to counter-attack the Allies after they had landed.

The defeat of Germany

It took a further eleven months after D-Day to defeat the Germans. This delay was due to the following factors:

- The Americans decided to advance slowly on a broad front rather than make a concentrated strike at the Germans, which might overstretch supply lines and risk Allied forces being cut off by a German counter-attack. The British did attempt to speed up the advance through the Arnhem operation of September 1944. Airborne troops were landed behind the German lines in the Netherlands in an attempt to outflank the German defences. The plan failed because the land troops were unable to link up with the paratroopers.

- Hitler took a final gamble on victory in December 1944, in an attack known as the Battle of the Bulge. He tried to repeat the success of the Ardennes operation of 1940 when the German armies successfully broke through the French defences, but this time against the Americans. American troops were taken by surprise and the Germans only narrowly failed to achieve a breakthrough. It took the Americans nearly two months to recover the area they had lost in the offensive.

In March 1945 Allied troops finally crossed the Rhine and moved into Germany. By this time Germany was on its knees, having been bombed around the clock and starved by the Allied naval blockade. The surrender was signed in northern Germany on 8 May 1945.

Although the Allied landings in Normandy and their subsequent advance played an important role in the defeat of Germany, the crucial area was probably the Eastern Front. It was in the Soviet Union that the German army had 90 per cent of its casualties.

Revision tasks

1 Make a copy of the table below about women and the war. Use key words to complete each column.

Key areas	Explanation
Industry	
Land Army	
Armed forces	

2 Did women improve their position as a result of their role on the Home Front? Draw up a balance sheet to illustrate your answer, showing progress and lack of progress.

3 Make a copy of the table below. Complete it using the information from this section to explain the events of 1944–45.

Event	Explanation
Preparations for D-Day	
D-Day landings	
Allied advance	
Why the Allied advance slowed down	

4 Using information from this section, make a list of reasons for the success of the landings on D-Day.

- free ante-natal clinics and maternity benefit for mothers
- a reduction in deaths from diseases such as tuberculosis and diphtheria
- dental treatment for 8.5 million people and spectacles for 5.25 million people in the first year alone.

However, it also brought problems.
- The NHS was very expensive to run. It cost £400 million in its first year.
- Others said that it encouraged people who wanted something for nothing and that taxpayers' money was being needlessly squandered.
- Some disliked the fact that there was still private practice. They argued that this would lead to twin standards and better care for those who could afford to pay.
- In 1951, the Labour Government introduced charges for spectacles, false teeth and prescriptions. Bevan resigned in protest, insisting that everything should be free.

Comment

Many of the measures introduced by the Labour Government were not new. For example, National Insurance built on the work of previous governments, especially the Liberals. The National Health Service was new though, and it showed the commitment of the Labour Party to the creation of a welfare state.

Revision tasks

Using the information on pages 98–99 and above, answer the following questions.

1 Draw a mind map showing the reasons for the Labour election victory of 1945. Put the reasons in order, clockwise, beginning with the most important at twelve o'clock.

2 Why was the Beveridge Report so important?

3 Make a copy of the table below. Use the information from this section to explain the measures introduced to attack want.

Measure	Explanation
Family allowance	
National Insurance	
National Insurance (Industrial Injuries)	
National Assistance	

4 Draw up a balance sheet for the NHS. Was the NHS a great success?

Exam practice

SOURCE F

An 83-year-old woman, interviewed in 1998, remembers the start of the National Health Service.

'When the National Health Service came in it was much easier to see a doctor, and it was free! My teeth had been bad since I had a baby and I was now able to have false teeth at no cost. They were sore at first but soon bedded in and became comfortable. Some of my friends got teeth because they were free but never used them. My mum got free spectacles and we all noticed how much better she could see.'

1 Use Source F and your own knowledge to explain why the National Health Service was popular. *(10 marks)*

Exam tip The Exam practice question on the left is an example of a question 3 from Unit 3. You need to:
- give a detailed explanation of what the source says about the popularity of the National Health Service
- add another reason from your own knowledge of why it was popular and explain it in detail.

Key content

You need to have a good working knowledge of the following areas.
Tick off each item once you are confident in your knowledge.

- ☐ the impact of the Depression 1931–39, including the growth of unemployment
- ☐ government measures to deal with unemployment
- ☐ the experience of the unemployed and the importance of the Jarrow Crusade
- ☐ the part played by the BEF, 1939–40, and the defeat of France
- ☐ the achievements and shortcomings of Dunkirk
- ☐ the importance of Churchill's leadership, 1940–41
- ☐ the importance of the Battle of Britain and the reasons for British victory
- ☐ the impact of the Blitz on Britain
- ☐ air raid shelters, the blackout and evacuation
- ☐ rationing, censorship and propaganda
- ☐ the changing role of women during the Second World War
- ☐ the D-Day landings and the defeat of Germany
- ☐ reasons for the Labour election victory of 1945
- ☐ the importance of the Beveridge Report
- ☐ the attack on want
- ☐ the setting up and immediate achievements of the NHS.

Check your knowledge online with our Quick quizzes at www.hodderplus.co.uk/modernworldhistory.

Chapter 9: The transformation of British society c.1951–79

Although this unit covers only 30 years of British history, they were times of enormous change. Britain in 1951 was recognisably much the same as it had been earlier in the twentieth century; by 1979 many of the key features of the Britain you live in today had been established. The changes affected nearly every aspect of the lives of the people of Britain: their education, their family life, their jobs and how they spent their leisure, who the British people really were and their attitudes towards each other.

Key topics

These are the key topics you need to revise. As with all examination topics you first need to learn the content so you know it well enough to answer a range of questions on this topic.

- British society and economy in the 1950s: an overview
- education, work and labour relations, c.1960–79
- media, communications and leisure, c.1960–79
- reasons for social change c.1960–79.

Starting points

In order to understand what changed, you need to know what the starting point was. Here are a few facts about Britain in 1951.

- The Second World War had ended only six years earlier. The British were proud of the heroic role their country had played in standing up to Hitler. Churchill, the wartime Prime Minister, had sat alongside world leaders Roosevelt and Stalin at the peace conferences.
- But the price of victory had been huge: 400,000 British people had been killed, including 60,000 civilians. Around 3.5 million buildings had been damaged or destroyed: many cities were still scarred by bomb sites. Britain had lost trade and was massively in debt. There were shortages of many kinds of foods and other goods, with wartime rationing and queuing still part of daily life. All young men had to do two years' **National Service** in the armed forces.
- Despite these difficulties the Labour government of 1945–51 had created a welfare state, including the National Health Service, providing support for British citizens 'from the cradle to the grave'.
- Britain still had an empire. India and Pakistan had become independent in 1947, but in Africa, the Caribbean and the Far East over 60 colonies were under British rule or accepted the British monarch (King George VI, father of Queen Elizabeth II) as their head of state.
- Very few families had a car, TV, telephone or fridge.
- The penalty for murder was death by hanging.
- Homosexual activity was a crime.
- Abortion was illegal. Having a baby outside marriage was a disgrace.
- Divorce was rare.
- Computers, the internet, mobile phones and DVDs had not been invented.

> ### Key term
>
> **National Service:** From 1949 to 1960 all males between 17 and 21 had to serve 18 months National Service in the armed Services (extended to 2 years in 1950).

> **Exam tip** When answering questions about change, remember to say what the situation was like at the start.

9.1 British society and economy in the 1950s: an overview

Although the 1950s were in some ways quite placid years, compared to what came after, the beginnings of change can be seen. There was almost full employment and, with a job and rising pay, many people were better off. Wartime restrictions disappeared and standards of living rose steadily. At the same time, the first major wave of non-white immigrants arrived to live and work in Britain.

Family, education and leisure

The war had disrupted everyone's lives. Fighting men had been sent all over the world, women were sent to work away from home and 3.5 million children were evacuated from their homes. In these post-war years most adults seemed to want to settle down to a quiet, traditional family life.

Men, women …

'Traditional family life' meant different roles for men and women. Victorian ideas of women as the 'weaker' sex lingered on: the man was expected to work, to be the family breadwinner. If they could afford it, women gave up work when they married and devoted themselves to housekeeping and looking after the children. Men were not expected to do much in the family home apart from a bit of gardening. Men dealt with the money; women handled the housekeeping but probably did not know how much their husbands earned. Many women did not have their own bank accounts.

Most men wore hats and were expected to raise them if they met a woman they knew. They were expected to 'watch their language' (not swear) in the presence of women. Men expected their wives to be virgins on their wedding day (in 40 per cent of couples, neither partner had any sexual experience before they married).

… and children

Children were expected to do as they were told and **defer** to their parents, particularly their fathers. The father was responsible for 'disciplining' the children, which might include hitting them. There was an obvious gender divide: boys played with toys such as construction kits and soldiers, while girls played with dolls and were expected to help their mothers with housework and cooking. Families ate their meals together, listened to the radio together, while children played with their toys in the family living room. On the other hand, children were allowed more freedom outside the home. Groups of friends would go off on their own for hours into the streets or the countryside.

> ### Key term
>
> **Deference:** a key word for this time. Women were expected to defer to men, children to adults, the poor to the rich, the less powerful to those in authority.

Education

Major changes had taken place in schooling following the 1944 Education Act. Instead of the all-through five to fourteen elementary school which most children had attended, there were now separate primary and secondary schools.

Children attended primary school from the age of five to eleven. Classes were often large, up to 40 pupils, and the curriculum focused on the basic skills of reading, writing and arithmetic.

At the age of eleven all pupils took a test, the 11+, to decide whether they should attend a grammar school or a secondary modern school. The test was supposed to measure intelligence but also to predict whether a child would benefit from the different curriculum at each type of school. Grammar schools had a more academic curriculum, usually including Latin, sciences and foreign languages, and prepared pupils for middle-class jobs. Secondary modern schools had a more practical curriculum, particularly as older pupils reached the leaving age, which had been recently raised to fifteen. The gender divide meant that boys did subjects like woodwork and metalwork to prepare them for the kinds of manual jobs they would probably be doing. Girls did subjects like cookery, needlework and typing to prepare them for their jobs and for home-building.

At the age of fifteen most girls and boys left school and started work. They then became part of the adult world, wore adult clothes and joined in adult leisure activities.

Leisure and entertainment

Only a tiny number of people had a TV in 1950, but 10 million radio licences were issued that year, the main source of home entertainment. The BBC's three channels – the Home Service, the Light Programme and the Third Programme – were the only ones available.

The great favourite entertainment of the British people was the cinema. Around 1.3 billion tickets a year were sold in Britain, 10 per cent of total world film audiences. Most towns had several cinemas, some of them quite luxurious, with cafés and an organist to play in the interval. The programme changed on Wednesday, enticing customers to visit the cinema twice a week. For as little as 2 shillings (10p), cinema-goers got a short film or newsreel, a 'second feature' or 'B picture' and then the main film. These were usually produced by Hollywood, but there were several British film studios too.

Professional sport had a huge following. There were 39 million attendances at league football matches in the 1950–51 season (in the 2011–12 season the figure was 16 million). County and test cricket, too, were far more popular than they are today. The British liked their sport: tennis, golf, bowls and angling clubs were the focus of social life in many cities, towns and villages.

Increasing numbers of people took an annual one-week holiday, usually by the seaside. Resorts were regional, with people from the Midlands going to Skegness and those from the north-west going to Blackpool (which received 17 million visitors a year in the 1950s). Families stayed in lodging houses, not hotels, were given just bed and breakfast and expected to be out all day. Walking holidays were also popular, especially for young people. The Youth Hostel Association had over 200 hostels – providing very cheap accommodation in scenic places – and more than 250,000 members.

Employment

Standards of living

Following the end of the Second World War, the United Kingdom enjoyed a long period of economic growth well into the 1950s and 1960s. Unemployment stayed low, only occasionally touching 2 per cent. This meant that jobs were plentiful and secure, with rising wages: in 1950 the average wage was £6.40 a week; by 1960 it was £11.12 and by 1964 £18 a week. These wages may seem pitifully low by today's levels, but beer cost 4p a pint, a small car was £80 and you could buy a decent house for less than £1,000.

While wages nearly tripled over this period, prices doubled, bringing about a steady increase in the **standard of living**. Spending on consumer goods rose by 52 per cent from 1952 to 1964. Homes before the war – many of them dating back to the nineteenth century – were cold, inconvenient and dirty with an unreliable electricity supply: only 88 per cent of houses in the UK had mains electricity at all. The 1950s Conservative governments set out to deal with the housing shortage by building new homes – 300,000 of them a year. These new houses were an improvement in many ways, and they all had mains electricity. This meant that there was a boom in demand for electrical household appliances, many of which had never been seen in ordinary homes before. From 1957 to 1959, the

> **Key term**
>
> **Standard of living:** the amount and quality of goods, housing, necessities and leisure activities people had.

number of washing machines sold rose by 54 per cent and fridges by 58 per cent. Significantly, it was the woman in the family who made the big decisions on these items as they would make big changes to her life. Women were therefore the targets of advertising, emphasising the time and effort the machines would save. The decision to buy a TV was probably a joint one and, at £60, a relatively expensive item, which is why many rented their first sets, at 48p a week. TV sales rose by 32 per cent. Car ownership changed people's lives, giving them the freedom to travel wherever and whenever they wanted. There were 2.5 million cars on the roads in 1952, 9 million by 1965.

Work

Working hours were long, often including Saturday mornings as well as Monday to Friday, but were nonetheless decreasing, from an average of 56 hours a week to 48 hours through the 1950s. Deference continued into the workplace, and workers were expected to be very respectful of their boss, foreman or supervisor.

Work was quite segregated by gender. Most men worked full time, often in manual work, in an all-male environment, doing hard, dirty, physical labour. Britain still had manufacturing industries, employing 8.7 million in 1950, and a coal-mining industry, employing 880,000. Employers would not think of taking on women to do these jobs and nor would women think of applying, even if they had done them in the war.

Most women faced a narrow range of jobs: shop assistants, laundresses, assembly line work in manufacturing and food processing, cleaning and, most of all in a pre-word-processing age, typing – in the 'typing pool'. Average women's pay was only 59 per cent of average male pay. The proportion of women who worked was steadily rising, up to 49 per cent of all women by 1957, but only 26 per cent of married women worked. The usual pattern was for a girl to work on leaving school, and perhaps continue after marriage, but as soon as she had children she, and the rest of society, expected her to stay at home and look after them and her husband. Only once their children had left home might an older woman take a job, probably part time. Women saw their pay as 'helping out the family income', or 'useful for those little extras'.

Exam tip Differences between how women and men were treated at work and in the home are often the focus of exam questions. Make sure you have plenty of examples.

Revision tasks

1 Make a copy of the table below and use it to summarise features of the lives of men and women at home and at work in 1950s Britain.

	At home	At work
Men		
Women		

2 Summarise the most important differences between the lives of men and women in two sentences each for 'At home' and 'At work'.
3 Use four to six words to describe the lives of children in 1950s Britain.

Immigration

There have always been black people in Britain, from Roman legionaries to Tudor musicians and sailors, and, when Britain became a major slave trade nation, black servants. But their numbers were few and were largely confined to London and the ports. This changed in the 1950s, as people from the Caribbean and south Asia took up their right to live and work in Britain. The reaction of some of the white population disturbed the relative calm of 1950s Britain.

British Nationality Act, 1948

The British Empire and Commonwealth gave their support to Britain in the Second World War. Alongside those from the old white Commonwealth (Australia, New Zealand, Canada, South Africa), thousands of people from Asia, Africa and the Caribbean joined up. For example, 10,000 West Indians joined the RAF.

After the war, Britain was forced to re-think its relationship with its colonies, moving them towards independence. The link with Britain would be kept through the idea of a 'Commonwealth of free and independent nations'. As part of this the British Nationality Act 1948 was passed, giving all Commonwealth subjects British citizenship. They had the automatic right to work and settle in the UK and to bring their families with them.

Over the next few years, immigrants began to take up this right, mainly from the Caribbean and the Indian sub-continent. One of the first groups to arrive came by sea on the *Windrush*, carrying 492 West Indians, mainly Jamaicans, who had paid £28 for the one-way trip. By 1962 some 300,000 West Indians and 160,000 Indians and Pakistanis had come to Britain. There are usually both 'push' (reasons to leave home) and 'pull' (expectations for a better life) factors for migration. For the West Indians they were:

Push factors

- There was a tradition of movement from the West Indies to seek work. This was often to the USA, but in 1957 the US government restricted immigration.
- The economies of the West Indian islands were in depression. Only 20 per cent of workers had full-time jobs, the rest had to make do with seasonal work. A large proportion of immigrants were skilled workers unable to find proper jobs at home.

Pull factors

- They had been taught at school that Britain was their 'mother country'. As we have seen, many had been to Britain in the war. They expected to fit in easily.
- The British economy was growing and was short of workers. Advertisements were placed in Jamaican newspapers, calling for women to come and work as nurses in the expanding National Health Service. London Transport also advertised, for example, hiring 3,500 employees from Barbados in 1956.

> **Exam tip** Remember to give several reasons why migrants came to Britain.

Reactions

Although the overall numbers were tiny, and many received friendly welcomes, the arrival of black immigrants revealed widespread racist prejudice and hostility. They were discriminated against in housing, jobs and in the streets. Landlords refused to let flats to black tenants, some blatantly, with notices saying 'No Blacks' in their windows. In other cases advertised accommodation would be mysteriously 'already let' when a black person applied. Some employers, often with the collusion of trade unions, operated a 'colour bar', not taking on any black workers, as in the case of the Bristol Bus Company. Those immigrants who were hired found themselves discriminated against, getting the worst jobs, with lower pay (28 per cent less, on average, than an equivalent white worker). Skilled workers were rarely able to use their skills, often having to take manual jobs; some graduate teachers, for example, had to work as bus conductors.

Racism sometimes turned to violence, egged on by **right-wing extremists**. In 1958 in Nottingham, a crowd of up to 1,000 fought with blacks. A few days later, in Notting Hill in west London, gangs of 300–400 white young men attacked local black people and their homes. In total 140 were arrested, but there were reports that police had been slow to react to black appeals for help. In 1959 a black carpenter, Kelso Cochrane, was murdered in London.

In the same year, Claudia Jones organised the first Notting Hill Carnival to give a positive image to black Londoners.

> **Key term**
>
> **Right-wing extremists:** (see key terms for 'right' and 'left' on page 108.) Extreme members of left or right are said to be on the 'wing'.

9.2 Education, work and labour relations, c.1960–79

By the 1960s and 1970s there was growing concern that while other countries were recovering well from wartime destruction, Britain was falling behind. Changes were made to increase educational opportunities and create a better educated nation. A lack of change in Britain's old-fashioned industries, as well as international events, produced crises and conflicts throughout the 1970s.

Changes in education

The end of the 11+

By the 1960s pupils in each type of secondary school were:

School type	Pupils (%)
Secondary modern school	62
Grammar school	28
Technical school *(The original idea was that there should be three types of state school, but this type, which was to have a technical bias to its curriculum, never really got going.)*	3
Independent school *(These schools are not funded by the state but mostly by fees paid by parents – often called 'public schools'.)*	7

The intention of this system was to pick out clever working-class children and give them the benefit of a good education, and for some it did. However, it was coming under criticism by the 1960s, for several reasons.

- The 11+ test was criticised as an unreliable indicator of future ability. Little allowance was made for 'late developers' who did not shine at eleven, and so failed to get a place at grammar school, but made progress later.
- Secondary modern schools had less money spent on them and lower expectations of the pupils, yet they were responsible for the education of nearly two-thirds of Britain's children. Marking so many children out as 'failures', at only eleven, often gave them a negative attitude towards education.
- In fact, grammar schools turned out to have an overwhelmingly middle-class intake: 60 per cent of middle-class children went to a grammar school, but only 10 per cent of working-class children. Working-class children at grammar schools sometimes struggled with a different culture, with parents unable to afford the hidden costs of trips and uniform, and pupils unable to cope with homework demands in a crowded home.
- From the **political Right**, the 11+ divide was criticised for producing a less well educated and so economically uncompetitive workforce.
- From the **political Left**, it was criticised as divisive, reinforcing class divisions and stifling the right of all children to a wider education.

In a few places experimental comprehensive schools had already been set up, taking all the pupils in their area, with no selection. Anthony Crosland, Minister for Education in the 1964–70 Labour Government, took the decision to expand the comprehensive school system. He instructed local education authorities to convert their schools to comprehensive schools through Circular 10/65. Putting this enormous change into effect took some years. Ironically, it was Margaret Thatcher, Education Minister in the Conservative Government from 1970, who was opposed to comprehensive schools but found herself having to approve many

Comment

The number of children who 'passed' the 11+ examination depended on the numbers of places available in the local grammar schools. This meant that in some areas as few as 10 per cent of all children went to a grammar school, but as many as 40 per cent did in others.

Key terms

Political Right and Left: political divisions are often labelled 'Right' or 'Left'. People on the Right hold strong beliefs in tradition, economic freedom and individualism. In the UK, the Conservative Party is the main party on the Right. On the Left, there are strong beliefs in equality, the protection of minorities and welfare. In the UK, the main party on the Left is the Labour Party.

comprehensive plans because they were too far advanced to be abandoned. By 1975 most areas had comprehensive schools, and today 90 per cent of young people in Britain are educated in them.

In 1973 the school leaving age was raised to sixteen in a further effort to ensure that Britain's young people were better educated.

Exam practice

SOURCE A

Historian Peter Clarke describes criticisms of the system of selective education.

'The fact was that secondary modern schools ended up preparing working class children for working class jobs ... This was the basis of the case for comprehensive schools.'

1 Use Source A and your own knowledge to explain why there was growing support for comprehensive education in the 1960s. *(10 marks)*

Exam tip The Exam practice question on page 107 is an example of a question 3 from Unit 3. You need to:
- give a detailed explanation of what the source says about the problems of selection at 11+, using your own knowledge to explain the context of the source
- add at least one more reason for support for comprehensive schools from your own knowledge and explain it in detail.

Universities

At the end of the war Britain had 26 universities, attended by 3 per cent of the population. The drive to expand higher education again came from two directions – the economic and the idealistic. Other countries had a much higher proportion of graduates and Britain had to increase university numbers in order to compete economically. At the same time, it was seen by many as élitist to restrict the opportunities of a university education to so few.

Eight new universities were planned and set up in the 1960s. Twenty-nine polytechnics were also set up, awarding degrees mainly in technical and scientific subjects, without all the facilities of universities. In 1960 around 200,000 students were at university; by 1969 there were 390,000.

The British economy, 1960–79

Up to the early 1960s the British economy was doing well:
- Growth was around 3 per cent.
- Unemployment was low – about 2 per cent.
- Inflation was usually under 5 per cent.
- The standard of living of the British people continued to rise. By the early 1970s nine out of ten British homes had a vacuum cleaner, three out of four had a fridge and two out of three a washing machine. In 1951 20 per cent of British homes had no indoor toilet; twenty years later the figure was only 4 per cent.

But there were underlying problems. Britain's economy was growing, but only at about 60 per cent of the rate of other economies, such as Germany, France and Japan.
- Britain had been the first country to industrialise, which had brought huge prosperity in the nineteenth century, but now its industries were old fashioned, lacking new investment in modernisation. The value of the plant which the average British worker used was £7,500; for the average German worker it was £23,000. In 1961 British production per worker was ninth highest in the world. By 1971 production per worker put Britain fifteenth in the world. This meant that British goods for export were often too expensive and therefore uncompetitive.
- British business was not good at finding and building up export opportunities. This brought about a 'trade gap', in which Britain imported more than was exported. This trade gap was £600 million by 1967.

- Britain was also dogged by old-fashioned industrial relations. In many industries workers' trade unions, were locked in conflict with managers.
- Britain had chosen to take on exceptional expenditure:
  - on defence, which took up 6 per cent of the wealth, more than most countries
  - on the welfare state. The National Health Service was costing £5,000 million a year by 1975.

These underlying problems emerged to bring about serious economic crises in the 1970s and 1980s as governments tried to deal with the linked problems of inflation, labour relations and unemployment.

Inflation

By 1970 **inflation** had risen to 6 per cent and continued to rise fast, peaking at 26.5 per cent in 1975. Workers demanded ever-increasing pay rises in order to keep up with, and even overtake, rising prices. In 1971 prices rose by 9 per cent and wages by 14 per cent: Britain seemed locked into a spiral of rising wages as both a cause and an effect of rising prices. In 1973 the sudden 70 per cent increase in prices imposed by oil producers (see page 110) worsened the situation.

Labour relations

Trade unions had become immensely powerful during the times of high employment and growth. Half of all male workers and a quarter of all female workers belonged to a trade union. Unions saw their role as getting the best possible pay and working conditions for their members. They were prepared to use strikes as a way of resisting any change which might lead to loss of jobs or pay for their members. Local trade union officials – shop stewards – could call a strike at short notice, bringing production to a halt. For their part, management hung on to their privileges and failed to build better working relationships.

Key terms

Inflation: a rise in prices over time. For shoppers, it means that money buys less.
Labour relations: the way managers and workers negotiate together, deciding on issues like wages, hours, etc.

Exam practice

SOURCE B

From a speech by Margaret Thatcher in 1979. At that time she was leader of the Conservative Party, later Prime Minister.

'What some unions are doing is ridiculous. One of the things which has knocked the country very badly is its record for unofficial strikes. Wherever I go abroad they say the same thing, "stop all those strikes and well buy your goods".'

1 What can you learn from Source B about strikes in British industry? *(6 marks)*

Exam tip The Exam question on the left is an example of a question 1 from Unit 3. You need to find at least two things that the source tells you (these are called inferences). Back up each one by pointing out details from the source.

Both Labour Governments (led by Harold Wilson 1964–70, 1974–76 and James Callaghan 1976–79) and a Conservative Government (led by Edward Heath 1970–74) tried to tackle the wage/price spiral, by calling for 'pay restraint', or passing laws to restrict strikes or by trying to reach agreement with unions. They were only partly successful.

- **1972 Miners' strike.** With 300,000 members, the National Union of Mineworkers was one of the most powerful trade unions, with committed members and some forceful leaders. When their pay claim was rejected they went on strike. Groups of miners prevented coal supplies from getting in to power stations by **picketing** the gates. At Saltley in Birmingham, pickets of Yorkshire miners forced the gates to be closed and power throughout the Midlands was cut to three days a week to conserve supplies. The Government agreed a 21 per cent pay rise for miners.

Key term

Picketing: used by trade unions during strikes. Members stand outside a place of work to try to prevent other workers from going in to work.

- **1973 Oil crisis**. The long conflict between Israel and the Arab nations erupted again in 1973 in the Yom Kippur War. The USA gave military support to Israel. In retaliation, the Arab oil-producing nations raised the price of oil, on which most economies were heavily dependent, by 70 per cent. This had a huge impact on most western economies, including Britain. Inflation increased even further.
- **1974 Three-day week and miners' strike**. The oil price rise increased the importance, and the price, of coal as the main alternative source of fuel. In November 1973 miners began an overtime ban in order to win a further pay increase by restricting the supplies of coal. Conservative Prime Minister Heath refused to back down and ordered a three-day week for most British industries, starting in January 1974. Most homes had to cope with no electricity for heating, lighting and cooking for several hours a day. In February 1974 the miners called an all-out strike and Heath called an election, demanding 'Who governs Britain?'. Labour won the election and awarded the miners a 35 per cent pay rise. Some 70 million working days had been lost to strikes during 1970–74.
- **1978–79 'Winter of Discontent'**. The Wilson (1974–76) and Callaghan (1976–79) Labour Governments were reasonably successful at reducing inflation – it was down to 8 per cent by 1978. Pay claims were to be held at 5 per cent or less. This was enforced on **public employees**, such as council workers and hospital staff, although workers in private industry often managed to win much more than this – workers at Ford's motor factory, for example, received a 17 per cent pay award and lorry drivers 20 per cent.

In angry mood, public service workers began a series of strikes in January 1979. The impact of their action was very visible: some hospitals closed for everything except emergencies, rubbish collections stopped and refuse piled up in the streets. In Liverpool grave diggers went on strike, so bodies went unburied.

These disputes were ended quite swiftly, but 29.5 million working days had been lost to strikes in 1979. The impression of being out of touch lost Callaghan the 1979 election to the Conservatives. Mrs Thatcher became Prime Minister.

> **Key term**
>
> **Public employees:** people who work providing a service for the public, rather than seeking to make a profit for a business. Public employees work for central government or local councils and include civil servants, teachers, nurses, doctors, police, refuse collectors, highway maintenance, postmen and firemen.

Unemployment

Having been low and steady at around half a million for twenty years, unemployment began to rise, topping 1 million in 1972. By the end of the 1970s 5 per cent of workers were unemployed. (This figure was soon to rise rapidly, reaching nearly 4 million, or 12 per cent, in 1984.)

All the factors dealt with above played their part in restricting British growth and shutting down businesses:
- Britain's uncompetitive industry
- failure to take export opportunities
- bad industrial relations, including strikes
- inflation
- oil price rise, 1973
- the three-day week, 1974.

> **Revision task**
>
> Make a copy of the table below and use it to summarise the reasons for rising unemployment through the 1970s.
>
> | | Description | How this factor led to increased unemployment |
> |---|---|---|
> | Britain's uncompetitive industry | | |
> | Failure to take export opportunities | | |
> | Bad industrial relations, including strikes | | |
> | Inflation | | |
> | Oil price rise, 1973 | | |
> | The three-day week, 1974 | | |

Exam tip Remember to give several causes for major trends that increased unemployment.

9.3 Media, communications and leisure, c.1960–79

Increased prosperity combined with new technology in the media, entertainment and leisure industries to bring radical changes to everyone's lives. Britain became world famous in the 1960s for pop music and fashion, with a reputation for creativity and flair, all focused on young people.

Changes in the media

Television

One of the biggest changes to everyone's lives in this period was the rise of television. In 1950 only 10 per cent of homes had a television set. The sets were in large cabinets, with a 12- or 14-inch screen. Programmes, in black and white, were transmitted from 3p.m. (5p.m. on Sundays) to 10.30pm, with a shutdown from 6–7p.m. so that parents could get their children to bed.

The coronation of Queen Elizabeth II in 1953 was televised, prompting many families to buy – or rent – a television. The BBC was the only channel they could watch until 1955 when the Conservative Government passed the Television Act, allowing 'commercial' television, ITV, paid for by advertisers. To make money from advertisers it was important for ITV to win over a mass audience, which they did with 'soaps' such as *Coronation Street* (first broadcast in 1960) and quiz shows such as *Double Your Money*. This had an impact on the BBC, which made more effort to gain mass appeal, splitting into BBC1 and BBC2 in 1964. BBC2 became the first colour station in 1967. By 1972 93 per cent of homes had a television and families spent a quarter of their spare time viewing.

Cinema

The rise of television had a huge impact on what had been the British people's favourite entertainment night out – the cinema. Attendances plummeted, falling to one-tenth of the 1946 peak by the end of the 1970s. All over Britain cinemas closed down, changing the look of British towns for ever.

Radio

Television also, of course, had a big impact on radio audiences. Over 10 million radio licences were taken out (at a cost of £1 a year) in 1954, falling to under 2 million by the late 1960s, until the radio-only licence was abolished in 1971.

The BBC still had a **monopoly** of radio broadcasting, by law, but was slow to react to the rise of pop music (see page 114) and the millions of people, especially young people, wanting to hear it. This demand was met by 'pirate' radio stations, operating offshore, from ships or disused forts, outside British law. Radio London (1964–67), Radio Caroline (1964–89) and Radio Luxemburg were the most popular, with teams of DJs playing non-stop 24-hour pop. The BBC eventually reacted and re-organised into Radios 1, 2, 3 and 4 in 1967, with former pirate radio DJs on Radio 1.

The decline of radio was not as total as the collapse of cinema-going. The invention of small, portable, transistor radios from the late 1950s enabled people to carry on with their lives while still listening. From the 1970s, many listened to car radios.

> ### Key term
> **Monopoly:** a monopoly exists when a person or organisation is the only supplier of something and there is therefore no competition.

Newspapers

Like so much of British life, the newspaper industry took a long time to recover from the war. Newsprint was rationed until 1956, so newspapers were short, about six to eight pages. The only **tabloid newspapers** were the *Daily Mirror* and the *Daily Express*. By twenty-first-century standards they were dull, with fewer advertisements, fewer pictures (none in colour), more politics and foreign news. The front page of *The Times* was simply a page of small advertisements until 1966. Nevertheless, more people bought newspapers than today. In 1954 the best-selling newspapers were *Daily Mirror*, 4.6 million copies a day, and the *Daily Express*, 4 million. In 2013 the best-selling newspaper, the *Sun*, sold 2.4 million copies a day.

Fierce competition for sales in the 1960s and 1970s changed newspapers so that they began to look more like they do today. Coverage of politics, and especially foreign politics, decreased in favour of more entertaining news items. Stories about the lives of celebrities, especially if they involved some scandal, became more common. There were complaints about such stories being an invasion of personal privacy as early as 1970. The leader in this move was the *Sun*, originally launched in 1964, but taken over by Rupert Murdoch and re-launched as a tabloid in 1969. It became Britain's best-selling newspaper in 1979, overtaking the *Mirror*.

The record industry

Record sales in 1950 were 189 million; in 1962, 687 million. The whole story, of the rise of rock 'n' roll, of teenage culture and British pop, lies behind these figures and is dealt with below. But the revolution in the pop music business could not have happened without technological changes.

The records sold in 1950 were 10 inches (25cm) or 12 inches (30 cm) in diameter, played at 78 revolutions per minute on a wind-up gramophone, with limited sound volume, lasting a maximum of five minutes. By 1962 the records were 7-inch (18cm) vinyl disks, played at 45 rpm on a record player, producing a better quality and much louder sound. Record players were designed to hold a stack of these. 'LPs' (Long Playing) records also appeared in the 1950s, played at 33⅓ rpm, taking several tracks and lasting at least 20 minutes. Stereo sound systems were available from 1958. Fans of all ages now had access to high quality music in their own homes, while teenagers had the music they wanted, loud enough for parties.

Revision task

Make a copy of the table below and use it to summarise the changes that took place in each of these media industries during the 1960s and 1970s, and their impact on everyday lives.

	What changed	The impact of changes on everyday lives
Television		
Cinema		
Radio		
Newspapers		
Records		

Key term

Tabloid newspapers: examples are the *Sun*, the *Mirror*, the *Express* and the *Mail* and they are smaller than 'broadsheet' newspapers (e.g. *The Times*, *Guardian* and *Telegraph*). They are aimed at a large, popular audience.

The 'Swinging Sixties'

The label the 'Swinging Sixties' was originally dreamed up by journalists and has been used ever since to describe the dramatic developments in British popular culture, especially music and fashion, which took place in the 1960s.

Music

Rock 'n' roll reached Britain from the USA in 1956 with Bill Haley's Film 'Rock Around the Clock'. For a while US stars, particularly Elvis Presley and Buddy Holly, dominated sales. The top five best-selling records of the 1950s were all by American artists.

However, in the early 1960s a wave of British bands took over, led by the Beatles: the top eight best-selling records of the 1960s were all by British artists. The Beatles formed in 1960 in Liverpool and also performed in Hamburg. They had their first number one hit, 'Please Please Me', in 1963 followed by seventeen more number ones over the next six years. Their first appearance on US television in 1964 was watched by 23 million households. Everywhere they went they were met by crowds of screaming girls, a phenomenon called 'Beatlemania'. Although heavily influenced by American rock 'n' roll, the Beatles produced many original songs. They were unconventional and creative, just the mood of the Swinging Sixties. Other bands from Liverpool, as well as London bands such as the Rolling Stones and the Kinks, were hugely successful, not only in Britain but across the world.

Fashion

The key British fashion item was the miniskirt, introduced by designer Mary Quant at her shop 'Bazaar' in 1964. Several inches above the knee, miniskirts were not only sexy but expressed a new freedom for women. Fashion shops in the King's Road, Chelsea and Carnaby Street drew visitors from all over the world. But these fashions were cheap, too, and soon every high street was selling miniskirts. Men's fashions rejected old restrictions too, favouring long hair, bright colours and flared trousers.

Culture

This was also a creative period for British art, films and theatre. The National Theatre began in 1963 and moved to its present building in 1976.

What made the Swinging Sixties possible?

Many other topics from this chapter contributed to the changes of the Swinging Sixties:

- Continuing prosperity and full employment meant that people had money to spend (see pages 105–106).
- Changes in the law made Britain a free-er, more tolerant society (see page 117).
- The culture of the Swinging Sixties, its music and its fashion, was above all a youth culture. The new phenomenon of 'teenagers' is described on pages 116–117.
- The critical attitude of young people towards older conventions is described on pages 122–123.
- The importance of the contraceptive pill in changing women's lives and young people's sexual relationships is described on page 124.

Critical attitudes

Whether the Swinging Sixties were a good or a bad thing for Britain is controversial. Critics have insisted that there was a down side to the freedom and experimentation. Drugs like marijuana and harder drugs became widely available and almost acceptable. Sexual liberation left unwanted pregnancies, and increases in abortions and divorces.

Was it just a media creation?

The phrase 'Swinging Sixties' was an easy slogan. It was taken up as a way of attracting visitors to Britain and by the end of the 1960s the King's Road and Carnaby Street were popular tourist destinations. Away from certain parts of London and certain small groups of people, life went on without dramatic change.

Nevertheless, it was impossible not to be affected by this time of new and exciting freedoms, creativity, and rejection of everything that was old and conventional.

> **Exam tip** Give a balanced view for best answers.

Revision tasks

1 Use six words to describe key features of the Swinging Sixties.
2 'Youth' was a central feature of the Swinging Sixties. Show how as many of your six words as possible link to youth.
3 Make a copy of the set of scales shown here. Write in the pans points you would make in support of each side of the argument about the Swinging Sixties.

Successes

Criticisms

Changes in leisure

By the 1960s most workers had one week's paid holiday a year. This usually meant a traditional seaside holiday, but changes were beginning to happen. One of the less attractive sides to staying in a seaside boarding house was that the landlady only provided bed and breakfast: you had to be outside all day, whatever the weather, and find your own entertainment.

An increasingly popular alternative was a holiday camp. There were already 200 holiday camps in Britain in 1939, but they grew in number and size through the 1950s and 1960s. There were fourteen Warner's camps by 1964 and ten Butlin's. At £2.50 per person per week, holiday camps were not the cheapest holidays, but some of the Butlin's camps had accommodation for 10,000 visitors. Families stayed in rows of chalets, and every part of every day was filled, from the loudspeaker announcing 'Good morning, campers!' to the end of the lively show in the camp theatre every evening. The huge, modern-looking restaurants served three meals a day. There was a swimming pool, a funfair, tennis courts and a dance hall. There were competitions, games and sports and plenty of indoor activities to cope with the British weather. Children were looked after by 'Redcoats' (at Butlin's), so parents could relax and enjoy themselves.

It was the British climate that brought the decline of British seaside holidays and holiday camps. From the 1950s onwards package holidays to the Mediterranean attracted increasing numbers. Only 1 million Britons took a holiday abroad in 1950; by the 1970s 10 million were doing so. The 'package' – flight, transfer and hotel – removed any anxiety about coping with foreign customs and languages. Cheap food, cheap booze and, most of all, guaranteed sunshine drew huge numbers, mostly to Spain.

Exam practice

Advertisement for Butlin's holiday camps, 1960s.

1 Study Source C. What was the purpose of this representation? Use details of the poster and your own knowledge to explain your answer. *(8 marks)*

Exam tip The Exam practice question on the left is an example of a question 2 from Unit 3. You need to explain what this poster is trying to make people think, or do. Refer to details from the source to support your answer.

Car ownership

By the 1960s many more people were able to buy a car. Cars such as the Mini and the Ford Cortina brought cheap motoring to the masses. By today's standards they were crude and uncomfortable vehicles, but the difference between family life with a car and without was huge. Car ownership made possible all sorts of day trips. Families were now free to travel anywhere in the UK. It opened up Devon and Cornwall as holiday destinations. Cars allowed ordinary people to discover new destinations, previously unthinkable by bus or train.

There were 4 million cars on the roads in 1950; 19 million by 1971. All this traffic on Britain's old-fashioned single carriageway roads brought terrible traffic jams, especially at weekends on roads to the coast. The first motorway opened in 1958 and, for a while, dealt with the jams.

Youth culture

The birth rate between 1946 and 1950 went up by 30 per cent, as couples who had been separated by the war got married and began families. The increasing prosperity (see pages 105–106) also encouraged couples to have children. This trend was called the 'baby boom'. These 'baby boomers' grew up in the 1960s to create a new culture: the teenager. Teenagers were healthier (because of the NHS), better educated (because of the 1944 Education Act) and free of the danger of war (National Service had begun to end in 1957). When they left school there were jobs for them, with decent pay and no one else to spend it on except themselves. It was calculated that teenagers had £850 million to spend each year, and businesses were quick to react. Around 40 per cent of all spending on records and 30 per cent of all spending on cosmetics came from teenagers. Teenagers had their own music, fashion (see page 114), shops and cafés. They had their own magazines and their own radio stations (see page 113).

Groups of young people identified themselves through their clothes. In the 1950s 'Teddy Boys' dressed in 'Edwardian' style, with long jackets, narrow trousers, thick-soled shoes and hair in a quiff. In the 1960s two groups emerged: 'Mods', who wore parkas and rode scooters, and 'Rockers', who wore leathers and rode motorbikes. Sometimes there were fights, as at Clacton seaside resort in 1964. Later conflicting groups were 'skinheads' and 'hippies'.

Exam practice

SOURCE D

A man in Coventry remembers how he spent his money when he was a teenager in the 1960s.

'Every week I'd buy at least two or three singles. I had so much money to spend it's unbelievable looking back. There were so many well-paid jobs for teenagers connected with the car industry. I'd spend ten pounds every weekend on myself, on clothes, on going out, and, most of all, on music.'

SOURCE E

From an article in the *Daily Mail*, October 1949.

'Teenagers are pampered with high wages, first class working conditions and excellent facilities in education. Their outlook is centred on trashy books and films. The boys are defiant and uncouth, while the girls are brazen and unrefined.'

1 How reliable are Sources D and E as evidence of teenagers in Britain in this period? Explain your answer, using Sources D and E and your own knowledge. *(10 marks)*

Exam tip The Exam practice question above is an example of a question 4 from Unit 3. You need to use your own knowledge to compare the reliability of *both* sources on the basis of:
- what is in the sources, what each one says
- the nature, origin and purpose of each source.

Reach a judgement about both sources by comparing the usefulness of each source in answering the question.

9.4 Reasons for social change c.1960–79

How laws were changed

In the early 1960s laws concerning personal behaviour were still much as they had been 100 years earlier. For example:

- Homosexual activity was still a criminal offence. Fear of the law caused grief and anxiety for gay people and made it impossible for them to lead their lives openly.
- Abortion was against the law, yet many illegal abortions were carried out each year, perhaps 200,000 of them. Some were in expensive clinics and some were 'backstreet' abortions, causing deaths and permanent injuries.
- Divorce was hard to obtain. One of the few grounds for divorce was adultery and some couples, who simply recognised that their marriage was over, would fake evidence of adultery in order to obtain a court judgement.
- Censorship. Books and plays could still be censored. By an Act of 1857, magistrates could still decide that a book was obscene and have it banned. By an Act of 1843, the Lord Chamberlain could ban a play.

In the 1960s all these laws were changed, as you can see below.

Reasons laws were changed

Important changes in the law both reflected and encouraged a desire for greater personal freedom, less interference in how people wished to lead their lives. At the same time the law was used to try to outlaw prejudice and discrimination by race or gender. The authority of the older generation and of men came under challenge from young people and women.

Legal reasons

When law makers changed these laws they gave the following:

1 The law was out of touch and no longer reflected the way people actually behaved. If a law is out of touch with reality it can make courts (who have to enforce the law) look ridiculous.
2 The laws were causing serious and unnecessary harm to individuals (for example, deaths from backstreet abortions, or mental anguish for gay people who had to hide their sexuality).

Underlying reasons

But beneath these were some more underlying reasons:

3 Loss of deference. A new generation was beginning to reject the deference of the 1950s (see page 104). The laws listed above belonged in the past, when people were expected to do as they were told. Many were coming to believe that it was not the job of the government to control people's private lives. They wanted to decide how to live their own lives.
4 Decline of religion. Religion was the moral force that lay behind some of these laws but its influence and authority was declining.

Enabling reasons

5 Individual politicians. Both parties accepted the need for more a **liberal** attitude, but it was Roy Jenkins, Home Secretary from 1965 to 1967 in the Labour Government of 1964–70, who put through many of the key changes affecting homosexuals, abortion and race relations.

> ### Comment
>
> *It is often difficult to give precise reasons for social change. Causes and effects can be confused or interconnected – for example, did changing social attitudes lead to changes in the law, or did the law change attitudes? Or both?*

> ### Key term
>
> **Liberal:** a 'liberal' (small 'l') attitude means more tolerant, free-er, open to change.

Censorship

Obscene Publications Act, 1959. This was introduced by Roy Jenkins before he was a Minister, just an ordinary MP. It allowed publishers to defend a book which might otherwise be considered obscene if it had artistic merit.

 Theatres Act, 1968. This abolished censorship of plays.

Homosexuality

Sexual Offences Act, 1967: Homosexual acts in private between consenting adults (i.e. aged over 21) were no longer a crime. The Act did not apply to Scotland and Northern Ireland.

Abortion

Abortion Act, 1967: Abortions were legal if doctors decided that continuation of the pregnancy would endanger the physical or mental health of the pregnant woman or any existing children of her family or if the baby was likely to be physically or mentally abnormal. The operation had to be carried out by a qualified doctor, and the foetus had to be less than 28 weeks old.

 The number of legal abortions rose from 4 per 1,000 live births in 1968 to 17.6 per 1,000 live births in 1975.

Race relations

Race Relations Act, 1968: See page 121.

Divorce

Divorce Reform Act, 1969: Couples could divorce after they had been separated for two years (or five years if only one of them wanted a divorce). A marriage could be ended if it had simply irretrievably broken down, without having to show that one of the partners was 'at fault'.

 The number of divorces rose from 2.8 per 1,000 married couples to 9.6 by 1975.

Reactions on the Right

Critics of these changes from the Right said that they created a permissive society. By this they meant that they gave permission for people to do what they wanted, irresponsibly, regardless of the effects of their actions. They say that easier abortion and easier divorce led to sexual promiscuity, single parents, decline in marriage and the breakdown of the family. Removing censorship also gave permission to writers and playwrights to use swear words and to portray sexual deviance, which also contributed to a lack of self-control. Mrs Thatcher, leader of the Conservative Party from 1975, joined in this criticism. Mary Whitehouse, motivated by her strongly Christian moral beliefs, founded the Viewers and Listeners Association in 1965. They particularly criticised the BBC for its portrayal of sex and violence and its bad language, and condemned homosexuality as deviant and immoral.

Reactions on the Left

Roy Jenkins rejected the term 'permissive society' and said he had created a 'civilised society'. Other critics pointed out that some of the new laws were only halfway points. Whether a woman had an abortion was still not up to her, but she had to persuade a doctor that her physical or mental health was in danger if she had the baby. The age of consent for heterosexuals was 16, but 21 for homosexuals.

 Changes in attitudes had helped to bring about changes in the law. However, there is evidence that these changes in the law also worked to change social attitudes. For example, in 1969 only 12 per cent of the population had a tolerant attitude to homosexuality; by 1983 the figure was 62 per cent. With the force of law behind the changes, opponents of change were perhaps made to feel out of step, while the social breakdown that they feared hadn't really taken place.

Comment

The defence of 'artistic merit' was used in the trial in 1960 of Lady Chatterley's Lover, *by D.H. Lawrence, originally published abroad in 1928. Some idea of old attitudes, in which upper-class men felt they had the right to decide what the lower classes and women could read, can be seen in the question put to the jury by the prosecuting barrister: 'Is it a book that you would … wish your wife or your servants to read?' Despite its explicit sexual descriptions, the jury decided that the book had artistic merit and should no longer be banned in the UK.*

The death penalty

From 1840 the only crime carrying the penalty of death by hanging was murder and it was being used less and less. Between 1900 and 1954 there were 7,454 murders, for which 1,210 offenders received the death penalty, of which only 632 were carried out. In 1947 a bill for abolition was passed by the House of Commons on a free (non-party) vote, but was rejected by the House of Lords.

Three cases in the 1950s helped to push opinion towards its abolition.

- **Timothy Evans, 1950**: Evans was illiterate and given to fantasies. He was hanged for the murder of his daughter on the basis of a 'confession', possibly dictated to him by the police. Three years later Evans' neighbour in the same house, John Christie, was found guilty of a series of murders, including that of Evans' daughter. This case made very clear the dangers of capital punishment in cases of miscarriage of justice.
- **Derek Bentley, 1953**: Bentley was a nineteen-year-old of very limited intelligence, who had taken part in a burglary in which a policeman was shot. Bentley's accomplice, Christopher Craig, had fired the shot, but was only sixteen years old, so could not be hanged. Bentley's conviction rested on his having shouted, 'Let him have it, Chris!' The prosecution argued that it meant 'Fire the gun', but it could have been telling him to hand over the gun. Two hundred MPs sent a petition to the Home Secretary appealing for a reprieve, but this was rejected.
- **Ruth Ellis, 1955**: Ellis was a night club manager who was hanged for shooting her lover who had ditched her. Even the judge appealed to the Home Secretary for a reprieve, as did a petition signed by 50,000 people, but both were unsuccessful.

Exam tip The Evans, Bentley and Ellis cases affected the debate about capital punishment.

All three of these cases increased doubts about capital punishment. Labour MP Sydney Silverman campaigned for years for abolition, with support from individual MPs of all parties, although public opinion remained in favour of capital punishment. In 1957 the Conservative Government passed the Homicide Act, restricting capital punishment to murder of a police officer, killing by shooting, murder while committing theft, or while resisting arrest.

There were such obvious contradictions in this Act that total abolition moved nearer. In the six years leading up to the 1957 Act there were 87 hangings, around fifteen a year; in the eight years from 1957 to 1964 there were 29, less than four a year. In 1963 and 1964 there were just four executions, in each case of two pairs of people both involved in the same crime. In 1965 the Murder (Abolition of the Death Penalty) Act was passed, suspending the death penalty for five years. It was finally abolished in 1969.

Divisions and conflicts

Race relations

The arrival of non-white immigrants in the 1950s had provoked social tensions and some outright conflict, with riots in Nottingham and Notting Hill (see page 107). It seemed that the British people, having ruled millions of black people in other parts of the world in the days of the Empire, were unable to adjust to the reality of some of them wanting to come and live in Britain.

In the debates about immigration there was underlying racism, even if the issues discussed – such as the numbers of immigrants, jobs, housing, cost to social services – were not apparently about race, or colour.

There were increasing calls to abandon the 'open door' policy for Commonwealth immigrants provided by the 1948 British Nationality Act. In a poll in 1961, 90 per cent of those asked favoured restrictions on immigration.

Government responses to public opinion were mixed: they needed to react to public opinion, but did not want to appear racist. Some governments, mainly Conservative but also Labour, passed laws restricting immigration. Sometimes these laws were more or less racist, treating black and white people from the same origin differently.

Labour governments accepted restrictions on immigration but tried to encourage tolerance and acceptance of cultural diversity by passing laws to prevent discrimination. Unfortunately these were often ineffective. The combination of discriminatory immigration laws and feeble attempts to make discrimination a crime appeared inconsistent.

The Conservative Government responded to popular views by passing the 1962 Commonwealth Immigrants Act. Unrestricted immigration was stopped and those who could enter Britain were:

- dependents of people already in Britain
- students coming to Britain to study.

Others had to apply for a voucher to enter:

- 'A' vouchers were for those with a specific job to go to.
- 'B' vouchers were for those with skills or qualifications that Britain needed.
- 'C' vouchers were for anyone else, and their number was restricted each year.

The Labour Government elected in 1964 accepted these restrictions but hoped to create a more racially tolerant society, accepting a new cultural diversity. Home Secretary Roy Jenkins passed the 1965 Race Relations Act.

- It was now illegal to discriminate on grounds of race in public places, such as restaurants, cinemas, pubs and hotels.
- It set up a Race Relations Board to deal with complaints of discrimination.

But:

- the key areas of housing and employment were not included
- the punishments for breaking this law were very light.

There was little sign in the next few years that this Act was achieving its aims of lessening discrimination. The Labour Government therefore passed the 1968 Race Relations Act, which banned discrimination in housing and employment, trade unions and advertising.

However, all that happened if discrimination took place was that the Race Relations Board investigated the complaint and tried to get the offender to stop discriminating. Only if they refused did the issue go to court. In the first year of the Act only one offender was put on trial.

Racial tension persisted through the 1960s and some politicians could not resist using racist support to win votes. In 1964 the Labour candidate in Smethwick, Birmingham, who was a strong supporter of the 'open door' policy, was defeated by an openly racist Conservative.

In 1968 Enoch Powell, a senior Conservative and former Minister of Health, made a number of speeches, calling for a complete halt to black immigration. He spoke about a black takeover, of a school with only one white child and a street with only one white inhabitant, an old lady. He said that he foresaw increased racial tension and prophesied 'much blood' unless urgent action was taken to cut immigration. The school and the old lady were never found and Heath, the Conservative leader, sacked him. However, his speeches, with their graphic language, won him lots of support.

Kenyan Asians

Powell's speeches inflamed an already tense situation over immigration. The former British colony of Kenya had a substantial Asian minority. There were fears that when Kenya became independent in 1963 the African Government would discriminate against Asians and whites, so the British government of the time offered them British passports. Serious discrimination did indeed begin in 1967, when many Asians were driven from their homes. About 7,000 decided to get out, and arrived in Britain. Another 80,000 held British passports and the press and some Conservatives called for an immediate halt.

Comment

*Ugandan Asians
In 1972 the African ruler of Uganda, Idi Amin, gave Asians 90 days to get out of the country. Some 27,000 fled to Britain and were given special permission to stay.*

The Labour Government claimed that 'a flood' of penniless immigrants would put too much strain on social services and so passed the 1968 Commonwealth Immigrants Act. Only those who were born in Britain, or whose fathers or grandfathers were born in Britain, were allowed in. This clearly racist (and sexist) law nevertheless had popular approval.

Back in government in 1970, the Conservatives went further and passed the 1971 Immigration Act:

- Commonwealth citizens had to have a work permit relating to a specific job in a specific place before they could enter Britain.
- They had to register with the police and after twelve months had to re-apply for permission to stay. They had to live and work in Britain for five years in order to stay here.
- Those who wished to return to their country of origin could ask to be **repatriated** at government expense.
- 'Patrials' – those with a direct personal or ancestral connection with Britain, and therefore almost certainly white – had the right to come to Britain and stay.

> **Key term**
>
> **Repatriated:** returned to the country they came from.

1976 Race Relations Act

Previous Race Relations Acts passed by Labour governments had been ineffective and appeared to be swimming against a tide of racist attitudes. This third Race Relations Act set up the Commission on Racial Equality. This had greater powers to deal with complaints and the authority to promote equality of opportunity and good race relations.

Revision tasks

1 Make a copy of the table below and use it to summarise the changes in immigration policy.

	Act passed by Labour or Conservative Government?	Reason why the Act was passed	Result of the Act
1948 British Nationality Act			
1962 Commonwealth Immigrants Act			
1968 Commonwealth Immigrants Act			
1971 Immigration Act			

2 Make a copy of the table below and use it to summarise the changes in Race Relations policy.

	Reasons why the Act was passed	What the Act did	Success or failure?
1965 Race Relations Act			
1968 Race Relations Act			
1976 Race Relations Act			

Class and social mobility

For the first half of the twentieth century Britain's class structure remained much the same. Social mobility – how much you could move out of the class you were born into – was not very great. Whether you were working, middle or upper class, most people did the same kind of jobs as their parents and married within the same class.

The 1960s and 1970s saw an increase in social mobility:

- The growth of prosperity in the 1950s affected all classes and began to fudge distinctions based on how much money you had.
- The number of manual working-class jobs decreased as British heavy industry continued its long slow decline. There was a growth in 'white collar' managerial and professional jobs. Together these meant that the working class shrank in numbers while the middle class grew.
- Comprehensive schools and a doubling of the number of university places opened up middle-class careers to the children of working-class parents.

Teenagers' protest

The growth of teenage culture included protest. They rejected the deference that had characterised their parents up to and through the 1950s. They were not prepared to be told what to do by the older generation and just wanted to be free, not least in sex; the contraceptive pill was available on the NHS from 1969, but much earlier from friendly doctors and clinics, especially at universities.

In many ways, teenagers' way of life – their clothes, their music, their sexual freedom – was a protest against the older generation. But some protests were more political, with left-wing students and activists such as Tariq Ali taking the lead. British students felt a strong link with young people's protests in the USA against the Vietnam War, through the protest songs of Bob Dylan, Joan Baez and others. In France in 1968 students and workers nearly brought down the government.

Vietnam

Protest against US involvement in the Vietnam War was not confined to young people, but students made up more than half the protesters. The Vietnam Solidarity Campaign organised large demonstrations outside the US Embassy in Grosvenor Square in 1968. There was some violence and several arrests.

Universities

Students in some universities demanded more say in their courses and how the university was run. When their demands were not met they organised 'sit-ins', occupying university buildings and halting teaching. Several universities were affected in the late 1960s, notably LSE (the London School of Economics), Sussex, Essex, Leeds and Birmingham.

These protests got a lot of publicity, but in fact by no means all students took part. Only 16 per cent of students took part in the sit-ins at Leeds University and only 7 per cent at Warwick University. Research at Liverpool University in 1969 found that only 1 per cent belonged to far left organisations, while 29 per cent were Conservative supporters.

CND

The other issue that brought large and regular protests was nuclear disarmament. The Campaign for Nuclear Disarmament (CND) was founded in 1958 in protest against nuclear weapons, which could bring destruction of all life on Earth. They argued that Britain's possession of its own nuclear bombs made the country less safe, because it became more of a target for the Soviet Union. CND organised a march every Easter from 1958 from London to the Atomic Weapons Research Establishment at Aldermaston on Berkshire. In 1960 at least 60,000 took part, most of whom were young.

In 1969, in an effort to bring teenagers more into society and to recognise their significance, Labour Prime Minister Harold Wilson lowered the voting age from 21 to 18.

Exam tip Remember the three issues for youth protest: the Vietnam War, universities and nuclear disarmament.

The changing role of women

The first women's movement had been the campaign for women's suffrage, with the limited aim of winning the vote for women. This succeeded by 1928, yet throughout the years from 1950 to 1979 there were never more than 29 women out of over 600 Members of Parliament. At the same time, women were still being paid less for doing the same work as men, rejected for certain jobs purely on gender grounds, and regarded by many men as inferior. Changes in education (see pages 108–109) meant that many more women had good qualifications, but when it came to getting promotion they found that after a certain point they hit a '**glass ceiling**', with men being preferred for top jobs. Clearly, equality for women was a long way from achievement.

Key term

Glass ceiling: a barrier to promotion which is unspoken and unexplained, therefore unfair.

Feminism

From the late 1960s and into the 1970s there was a 'Second Wave of Feminism', taking the campaign for equality and fair treatment into many areas of women's lives.

Women's liberation

Many women joined the 1960s protest movements described above, driven by the same anti-authority motives, only to find that male leaders, however politically radical, expected women just to make the tea and type their manifestos. Women began to meet in women-only groups to discuss their anger at being marginalised in so many aspects of a male-dominated society. There were 70 such women's groups by 1969 and in 1970 the first National Women's Liberation Conference was held. This identified four key demands:
- equal pay
- equal opportunities in education and careers
- free contraception
- free 24-hour childcare.

Women's Liberation was a movement that included several different campaigns. Some wanted to show up **male chauvinism**. Others challenged sexual stereotypes. The Miss World contest in 1970 was disrupted by women protesters, arguing that such events promoted an image of women as objects. Others worked to outlaw discrimination against women through the law.

Key term

Male chauvinism: a belief that men were innately superior.

Employment rights

Women workers, usually much less militant than men, began to demand their rights. In 1968 the women sewing machinists at the Ford car factory in Dagenham came out on strike because they were classified as 'unskilled', and so received less pay than men who did the same job. Following the intervention of Barbara Castle, Minister for Employment in the Labour Government, the strike ended after three weeks. The women's pay was raised to 8 per cent below that of men, rising to full equality the following year.

Comment

The journal Spare Rib *began in 1972 to focus and spread feminist ideas.*

The different campaigns brought about significant changes to the law, and had some success:

- **Equal Pay Act, 1970**: People doing the same job should get the same pay, as well as pension rights, holidays, bonuses, etc.
- **Sex Discrimination Act, 1975**: No distinction to be made on grounds of gender, in recruitment, promotion or other rights. It also put an end to 'boys' subjects' and 'girls' subjects' in the school curriculum. The Act also set up the Equal Opportunities Commission to investigate discrimination and promote equal opportunities.

Contraception

The availability of the contraceptive pill, had equally long-term effects on the lives of women in Britain. The pill, along with the 1967 Abortion Act (see page 118), gave millions of women control over their sexuality. They could enjoy sexual relationships on an equal basis with men. They could plan when to have children, and balance family and career on their own terms.

Exam practice

SOURCE F

From a textbook published in 2013.

'Most of the best-selling women's magazines seemed blithely unaware of feminist thinking. Around 60% of articles in the three leading women's magazines in the 1960s were on the themes of "Getting and Keeping Your Man". A survey of Honey [a magazine targeted at young women] readers in 1978 showed that what they truly wanted was "a husband, a home and two children".'

1 Source F suggests that feminism made very little difference to women's lives. How far do you agree with this interpretation? Use your own knowledge, Source F and any other sources from other textbooks which you find helpful to explain your answer. *(16 marks)*

Exam tip The Exam practice question on the left is an example of a question 5 from Unit 3. You need to:
- use Source F, other sources and your own knowledge to agree with the statement
- then use other sources and your own knowledge to disagree with the statement
- comment on the reliability of each source in order to judge the strength or weakness of each side of the argument
- reach a balanced judgement on the interpretation.

Key content

You need to have a good working knowledge of the following areas.
Tick off each item once you are confident in your knowledge.

- ☐ British society and economy in the 1950s
- ☐ immigration push and pull factors and reactions
- ☐ changes in education
- ☐ the British economy, 1960–79, inflation and labour relations and unemployment
- ☐ changes in the media
- ☐ the 'Swinging Sixties' and what made them possible
- ☐ changes in leisure
- ☐ changing social attitudes and changing laws, including reasons why laws were changed
- ☐ divisions and conflicts
- ☐ the changing role of women.

Check your knowledge online with our Quick quizzes at www.hodderplus.co.uk/modernworldhistory.